KU-426-649

EFFORTLESS ENTERTAINING

EFFORTLESS ENTERTAINING

Simone Sekers

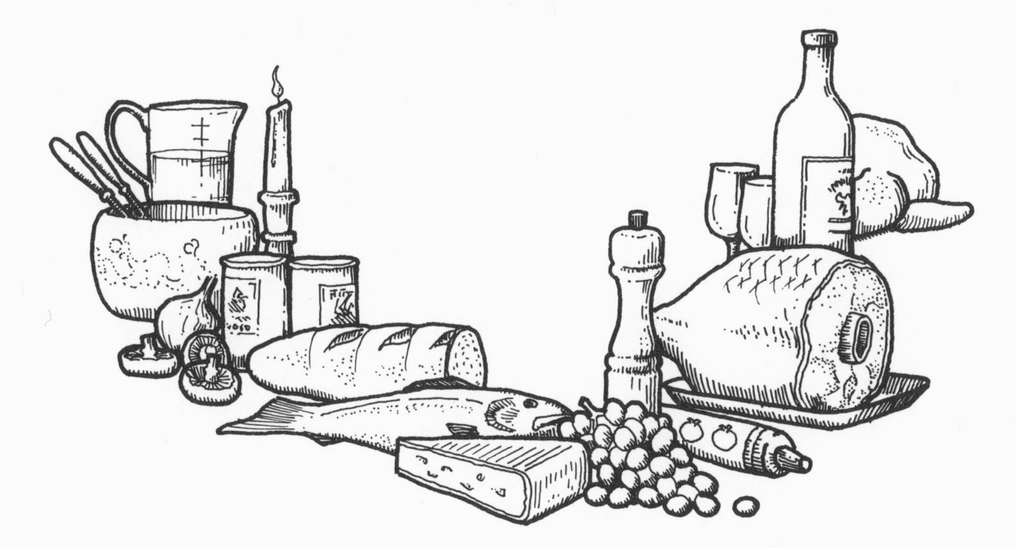

PIATKUS

This book is dedicated
to my entertaining family and friends,
with grateful thanks.

'One may often find round a single table all the modifications which extreme sociability has introduced into our midst: love, friendship, business, speculation, influence, solicitation, patronage, ambition, intrigue; that is why conviviality affects every aspect of human life, and bears fruits of every flavour.'

Jean-Anthelme Brillat-Savarin (1755–1826)
La Physiologie du Goût

First published in 1984
by Judy Piatkus (Publishers)
Limited of London

Designed by Susan Ryall

Drawings by Marcel Ashby

Typeset by Wyvern Typesetting Limited, Bristol

Printed and bound by
Mackays of Chatham Ltd.

British Library Cataloguing in Publication Data

Sekers, Simone
Effortless entertaining.
1. Entertaining 2. Cookery
I. Title
641.5168 TX731

ISBN 0-86188-094-3

CONTENTS

INTRODUCTION 7

BE PREPARED 11

GADGETS 15

WHEN, AND WHERE, TO ENTERTAIN 19

FIRST COURSES 21

One-step soups 21
Fish, meat and egg dishes 27

MAIN COURSES 39

Fish 39
Meat 49
Poultry and game 63
Informal entertaining 73

VEGETABLES AND SIMPLE SALADS 79

DESSERTS AND PUDDINGS 95

STORE CUPBOARD 107

PARTY DRINKS 113

SUGGESTED MENUS 115

STOCKISTS 125

INDEX 126

INTRODUCTION

For most people entertaining is feeding friends, and part of the pleasure of inviting friends to a meal is preparing something rather special for them to eat and enjoy. But don't for one moment think that cooking a three-course dinner or concocting a buffet or after-the-theatre supper need involve you in days of anxious preparation. The aim of this book is to make entertaining as effortless as possible. It is a recipe book for the person who is frequently short of time, but who nevertheless likes cooking and wants to produce good food with the least amount of fuss.

The dinner party is the way most people choose to entertain their friends and colleagues, and the majority of recipes I give can be prepared and finished off in the time between returning home from work and the arrival of the first dinner guest. There are recipes to suit every occasion and timetable, and I also include a selection of menu ideas at the back of the book.

The secret of successful and relaxed entertaining is good organisation. Cooking ahead, keeping a well-stocked freezer and a well-stocked store cupboard are the three basic rules I follow. Give yourself time to create a pleasant atmosphere for your guests – and enjoy their company.

Few of us escape having to entertain altogether, and many of us love it. Whichever category you fall into, the following points will be useful.

Planning the menu

1. Always keep a basic 'wardrobe' of classic ingredients in the freezer, if you have one. Chickens, legs or shoulders of lamb, braising beef, mince, chops, cod, trout, etc. are fairly standard family fare and can be dressed up with 'separates' such as eggs, cheese, pasta and vegetables. 'Accessories' in the form of flavourings and seasonings can be added to give the finishing touches.

2. Plan your menu round the main course, making it as simple or as complicated as the occasion demands. Whatever you choose, make the other courses slot neatly into place like a jigsaw: an elaborate main course needs a trouble-free first course, but a good-tempered casserole can be preceded by something as demanding as Mushroom and Prawn Croûtes (page 32).

3. Never be tempted to serve more than three courses. In fact, there are many occasions when a selection of cheeses and fresh fruit makes the perfect end to a meal.

4. Try planning a series of menus to suit various occasions at various seasons, then you can draw on them when inspiration deserts you. (See my suggestions on pages 115 to 124.) Keeping a small notebook and recording what you gave whom when will save duplication.

5. Plan your menu around your china cupboard; that is, don't have two courses requiring your only set of bowls, or one which demands teaspoons fore and aft when you only

possess six altogether. This may sound elementary, but it is easily forgotten when planning an exciting menu.

6. Use whatever is in season – it saves so much time to buy what is readily available, rather than hunting for strawberries in January or leeks in June.

7. It is a nice idea, and also a time-saving one, to make use of local specialities when menu planning; for example, potted shrimps, Cumberland sausage, smoked trout, clotted cream.

8. Fresh herbs make ordinary food memorable, so try growing at least one or two in pots on the window-sill if you do not have a garden. Chervil and chives are the easiest to grow, then come mint, thyme and marjoram, sage and rosemary. Basil (an annual) and tarragon need warmth and are slightly more trouble, but well worth it. You can usually buy parsley, which is the most temperamental to grow, and it freezes well.

9. Plan your menu around the space available in your kitchen. If you decide to prepare food in advance, make sure that you have enough storage space in your refrigerator.

10. Plan menus that do not involve too much washing up. Wash up as you go along. The recipes I give use as few dishes and pans as possible.

Choosing the wine

11. A well-stocked wine cellar is a good investment, in terms of time as well as money, although I am not talking about château-bottled claret but good reliable everyday wine. I have proved to myself over and over again that the two best sources of supply are Marks & Spencer and Sainsbury's, who both stock ranges of consistently good, reasonably priced wines. Even my husband, who knows a good deal about wine but who has even less time than I do to go out and look for it, is quite happy to leave me to choose from either of these stores. Decant the wine if you want to hide the label. If you do not have either of these shops within easy reach, it is well worth making a special trip and laying in a stock.

An American custom well worth adopting is to have tumblers and a jug of iced water on the table throughout the meal so that guests can help themselves.

12. After the meal always serve freshly ground coffee, and offer special mints or truffles if you like. But do not feel that you have to offer brandy or liqueurs unless you are having a formal dinner party or entertaining business acquaintances. Many people prefer to have another glass of wine.

The dining table

13. Remember that candlelight covers a multitude of sins, and that hoovering and dusting

are less important than a few fresh flowers, a pretty tablecloth and generous tablenapkins (whether paper or cloth doesn't matter as long as they are large), and lots of candles to cast a flattering and soothing light. Matching china is not important either if the colours blend. Aim for harmonious informality rather than starched uniformity.

14. Try to avoid cramped eating conditions if you can. Keep table decoration to a minimum, or remove altogether, and serve from a side table.

The guests

15. If you are entertaining mid-week and you and your guests have to work next morning, try not to allow too much drinking time before dinner – 20 minutes to half-an-hour always seems about right. Invite known late-comers well before everyone else so that there is some chance they will arrive on time.

16. Don't offer too many salted nuts and pretzels – unless you need to take the edge off your guests' appetites. And remember, the saltier the nuts, the more alcohol will be drunk.

17. Unexpected or extra guests can cause problems in the kitchen. It may be a case of 'family hold back', or cooking extra pasta, rice or vegetables to add bulk to the meal. In real emergencies try adding a little sherry to a good-quality canned soup, or have some of the store-cupboard recipes (pages 107 to 112) to hand.

18. Getting people to leave is not always easy, and simply yawning is a little heavy-handed, although it can be resorted to in emergencies. Offering soft drinks at a decent interval after everyone has finished with coffee and brandy or wine is a useful signal pounced on by the tactful.

19. Above all, relax and do not panic. Entertaining is not putting on an act, it is simply feeding friends.

***Note:* Quantities given are for 4 generous helpings.**
Use either the imperial or the metric measures in each recipe, but not a combination of the two.

BE PREPARED

The well-dressed career woman, urge magazines and the women's pages of newspapers, has one or two good classic outfits which can be juggled about with a few well-chosen separates and lots of accessories to provide a multitude of ensembles for every occasion. This works even better with food, especially if your working day does not give you time to shop specifically for a dinner party or for entertaining guests for a weekend. Here is the basic principle of the well-dressed larder (or freezer) fleshed out with some examples. Once you get into the rhythm of this way of shopping and cooking, it is the easiest thing in the world to top up once a week at a good supermarket, and to be prepared for anything.

The Basics

Lamb:
legs and shoulders; best end of neck (chined, so that it can be split up into chops); loin chops.
Pork:
almost every bit of the pig is useful, but chops, fillet, roasting joints, belly pork (for pâtés) and bacon joints are the best basic cuts.
Beef:
wing rib (the best roasting joint apart from sirloin); fillet; shoulder steak and shin for casseroles; mince.
Poultry:
chicken, whole and in joints; a duck or two; a small turkey or capon.
Game:
pheasant; grouse; venison; hare and rabbit.
Fish:
cod; coley or haddock; smoked haddock; trout.

It is worth buying your roasting joints from a reliable butcher, checking as you do so that they can be stored in the freezer and that they haven't been frozen before. I like to 'hang' my meat by storing it in the fridge for a day or two longer before freezing it, to make sure that it is tender. Always take advantage of supermarket special offers, especially on the cheaper cuts and on poultry – just after Christmas is often a good time to buy a turkey, for instance, and midsummer prices for stewing beef and pork roasting joints are lower than winter ones, when these cuts are in greatest demand. Game definitely needs to be well hung before freezing.

As for fish, it is becoming more and more difficult to buy good quality, spanking-fresh fish and shellfish in the provinces. If you can buy a box of fish at the quay, and freeze that, you will end up with a very superior product indeed. Otherwise, your freezer will let you take advantage of anything good on the fishmonger's slab when you happen to be passing.

The Separates

These will make quick meals in themselves.
Eggs:
supermarket ones for general recipes, free-range for specific egg dishes (don't store

them in the fridge, or you will have to remember to remove them to room temperature well before using them; an egg-rack is useful and decorative, and wall-hung ones are available if you are short of space).

Cheese:
this keeps well in the freezer, so you can take advantage of a really good farmhouse Cheddar by buying a large quantity (wrap it up very thoroughly so that the cold doesn't dry it out too much); buy cheaper cheese for cooking, and grate a pound or two to have ready in the freezer – it won't need defrosting before use.

Pasta:
in varying shapes; also lasagne and tagliatelle.

Rice:
brown, long-grain and Italian (known as 'easy-cook' in some brands, but check that it is not American; the grains should be short, fat and translucent).

Vegetables:
the best frozen vegetables are peas, spinach and stringless beans; dried peppers and mushrooms are useful.

Pulses:
green flageolets, haricot beans, chick peas, and brown lentils – health-food shops are the best sources of supply, especially the ones that deal in bulk (university towns usually have good cheap ones).

Fruit and nuts:
again, go to a health-food shop for such dried fruit as hunza apricots, Chinese peaches, etc.; citrus fruit and apples; some canned fruit; almonds, walnuts for puddings and decoration.

Accessories

Seasonings:
peppercorns and other whole spices, like cinnamon sticks, nutmegs, ginger root, cloves, and vanilla pods; have curry paste rather than powder if you can, and other whole Indian spices – coriander, cardamoms, star-anise, etc.; fresh green ginger, when available, can be stored, peeled, in a jar of sherry in the fridge (the sherry can be used as a flavouring in its own right); tubes of tomato concentrate.

Herbs and garlic:
try growing as many fresh herbs as you can (dried herbs, particularly commercially-dried ones, tend to add mustiness rather than flavour, with the exception of bay-leaves); garlic, and onions for that matter, are best stored in a picturesque basket or net so that the air can circulate round them.

Alcohol:
red and white wine, vermouth, cider, madeira, marsala, brandy and kirsch are the most useful.

Bottles and jars:
bottled fruit, useful for instant puddings (and worth making your own if you have time); herb flavoured vinegars; various mustards; mushroom ketchup; anchovy essence; Worcestershire sauce; tomato ketchup; olive oil and sunflower oil, pickled cucumbers, capers, olives, pesto (basil paste).

Cans:
anchovies; olives; tuna; crab and other shellfish; consommé; chestnut purée; frankfurters; prosciutto (surprisingly good in cans); black cherries; pineapple; sweetcorn; choucroute (or sauerkraut); good-quality canned soup; Italian plum tomatoes; ratatouille.

None of the above needs to be stocked in large quantities, although I tend to build up stocks of things like tuna, anchovies and olives, which are particularly versatile. The alcohol can equally well be stocked in the drinks cupboard, but you will probably use cheaper brands of madeira, brandy, cider and wine for cooking than you might for drinking. Miniatures of liqueurs are useful for desserts.

This 'wardrobe' is simply a list of the things that I find most useful, and can of course be varied to suit all tastes. I add any item I use during the week to my next shopping list so that the basic stock remains constant.

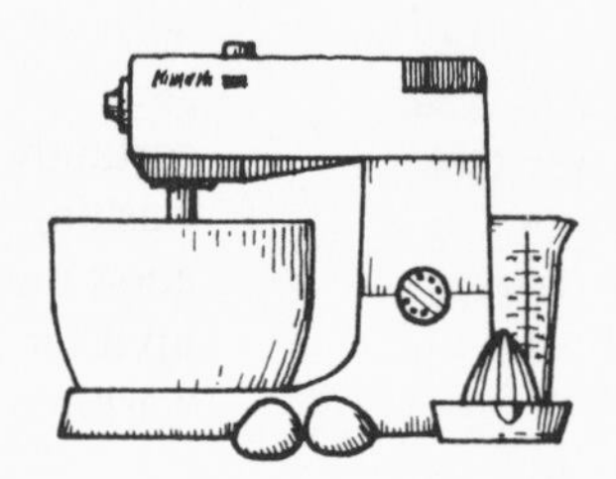

GADGETS

The four corner-stones of my kitchen are the food processor, the slow-cooker, the salad-spinner and the dishwasher, all of which are in more-or-less continuous use.

The food processor
I am a late convert to the *food processor*, but like most converts embrace the new faith with zeal. It really does reduce former chores to a minimum, and encourages me to try out recipes which previously had seemed beyond me – like quenelles, for instance. I still find my electric whisk indispensable, however; it can be used in pans on the stove, and is easy to clean.

The slow-cooker
does everything that the slow oven of a solid fuel cooker does, but for those of us who do not have a solid fuel cooker, it means the possibility of the really slow simmering that so improves a stew, without enormous fuel bills. And since cooker manufacturers seem to find it impossible to make a ring which has this ability to cook things *gently*, a slow-cooker is invaluable. I put stews in just before going to bed, and decant the cooked stew into a clean casserole in the morning knowing that it will be ready for that evening's dinner. Alternatively, I leave one cooking while I am working, safe in the knowledge that it won't burn or boil dry.

The salad-spinner
– one of those that looks like, and works on the same principle as, a spinning-top – is not only useful for preparing a salad and drying it without bruising, but for leaving the salad-stuff in perfect condition until the time to use it.

The dishwasher
is not an impossible luxury (I would far rather have one than a tumble-dryer), but a vitally useful boon in a busy life, and one which certainly does away with the dread pile of washing-up which is the bathos of so many a good dinner-pary. It is noisy, and it does take up a lot of room (but so do piles of washing-up), but I would rather do without the food processor than have to wash up all weekend when I have friends to stay.
Other equipment is more obvious:

A good range of saucepans, from egg-boiling to pasta-cooking in size. Nothing is more time-consuming than finding that a saucepan is already in use. Heavy cast-iron casseroles with enamel linings (Le Creuset is my favourite make; I still have two in constant use which were wedding presents fifteen years ago) can double as saucepans.

Oven-to-tableware – very useful as it saves on washing-up.

At least two gratin dishes, in both cast iron (or stainless steel with a copper bottom) and porcelain. Porcelain conducts heat best of all the types of pottery, and is very hard-wearing due to its high firing, so it is well worth the extra expense.

Ovenproof terrine.

A heavy baking-sheet; a spring-form cake tin with a removable base and an alternative ring mould base; at least two flan-tins with removable bases (china flan dishes look attractive but do not bake pastry well, so choose metal flan tins which fit neatly into the china ones – cook in the metal and serve in the china); a Swiss roll tin may be useful.

Good scales, with both metric and imperial weights shown. Beware of square scale pans with sharp corners, as they are difficult to clean. Old-fashioned scales with weights are still the easiest to use, but do take up a lot of room.

Two measuring jugs, again graded with both kinds of measurements, and a set of measuring spoons.

Sharp knives in varying sizes; a knife-sharpener and a rack to keep the knives handy and to stop them jostling together in a drawer, which blunts them.

Lots of wooden spoons (and a wooden fork, for stirring rice and pasta), a rubber spatula, a basting spoon and a straining spoon, a balloon whisk and a pair of sharp kitchen scissors – all can be kept in a jar beside the cooker, within easy reach.

Two colanders – a really large one for draining pasta, and a smaller one for general use. I find cheap plastic ones just as good as any others, provided they don't come into contact with the stove.

A food-mill and electric whisk are still useful, even if you do have a food processor. The food-mill is wonderful for purééing and straining at the same time, which means less preparation at the start of cooking (apples for a purée need not be peeled or cored first, for example), and the whisk makes short work of beating egg-whites, cream, and even mashed potatoes.

A hand-operated mincer is a cheap and useful gadget if you do not want to invest in a food processor, although the latter does treat meat more kindly, by chopping it rather than mincing and squeezing the juices out of it. Remember to chill liver and gelatinous meat such as belly pork and shin beef before mincing as it will make the whole job much easier. Better still, freeze the meat briefly so that it is really firm but not solid.

The microwave cooker still has its place, most usefully, in batchelor kitchens and restaurants, where its qualities of rapid defrosting and reheating are most appreciated. For the rest of us, the disadvantages probably outweigh these advantages – roasts and pastry emerge cooked but palid; great care has to be taken not to reheat anything in foil containers, or even to use china with gold or silver decorations, or you will be greeted with showers of sparks, and you will lose valuable worktop space. The best use we made of one recently was for drying glass-cloths while washing up after a Christmas dinner for seventy old people – the microwave managed that better than it did the reheating of the mashed potato!

A pressure cooker. Although I have one, I use it for only three things – a particular marmalade recipe, boiling Christmas puddings, and cooking beetroot. It should have a place in making entertaining effortless, but I honestly cannot think of one – stews taste far better when cooked slowly in a slow-cooker, as does any meat. Root vegetables, especially potatoes, are so unpredictable that within the cooking time advised by the manufacturers one variety of potato can cook to a glutinous mass, while another remains rock hard.

Ceramic pastry-beans, for baking pastry-cases blind; Bakewell paper, for lining cake-tins and helping to produce trouble-free meringues; a store of old, clean handkerchiefs for tying up spices etc.; string, and wooden skewers for binding meat and poultry; foil and cling film.

At least two good pepper-mills, in which the central spindle is held steady at the top by a metal or plastic bar. Unscrew the mill before you buy it, as many do not have this feature, and it really does help the grinding cogs at the bottom to last longer. I have one for pepper and another for coriander. Another indispensable gadget is a nutmeg grater, with a compartment at the back for the nutmeg.

Finally, *some sort of timer* – the ones that come on a string to hang round your neck are the most useful as you can take them with you without the risk of leaving them in odd places round the house. And if you have an automatic oven-timer on your cooker which you have never bothered to use, then find the instruction book and brush up on how to use it – it's the greatest asset the busy cook has. A delicious hot meal can be waiting on your return from the cinema, or you can go to the pub knowing that the oven will switch itself on, cook the food and switch itself off again if you are delayed.

Note – invest in the best, and the best in quality and value can most often be bought from professional catering supply shops, rather than trendy shops for the weekend cook, or from cookery departments in large stores.

WHEN, & WHERE, TO ENTERTAIN

The ultimate in entertaining is six good friends seated round a *round* table over a simple but carefully composed meal; the nadir seems to me to be a crowded buffet where the food consists mainly of rice and the drink of vinegar, and there is nowhere to sit.

'Dinner-party' has a rather formal sound, however, and I think most of us would rather call dinner 'supper', to avoid the black tie and silver candlestick image. But whatever you call the occasion, the idea is to make your friends feel welcome and somewhat pampered; buying some fresh flowers on the way home (not hot-house roses, but cheap and cheerful anemones) and arranging them swiftly in a vase, sorting out a pretty tablecloth and napkins, lighting candles, even lighting a real fire if you have one and the weather calls for it, are all quick and simple things that show you care. Try not to entertain more people round a table than you really have room to seat comfortably, with plenty of elbow room. If your table is very small, and you know a DIY enthusiast, it is possible to make an extra, larger, top from plywood, hinged down the centre so that it can be folded and stored under a bed or at the back of a cupboard when not in use. Some method of fixing it firmly to the table top is needed, but this can be done by using Blu-tak or even double-sided sticky tape if you are not worried about the table's surface.

Entertaining in large numbers can be fun, and a buffet meal certainly pays back a lot of hospitality in one go. Make sure that there are enough chairs for everyone, and, if possible, a number of small tables. It is surprising how many card-tables even a small room will hold, and these can often be borrowed or hired, along with chairs, from your local church hall or youth club. Aim at a bistro atmosphere, with each table covered with a cloth (Laura Ashley's remnant box yields useful lengths if you want to have a permanent supply; otherwise checked paper cloths look effective), add a candle and a litre bottle of wine, four brightly coloured napkins and four wine glasses – few card-tables hold more than four comfortably. Try to avoid paper plates and mugs if you can – they bend . . . Let each guest pick up his cutlery with his food, which can be of the simplest: a hot casserole with garlic bread, one or two salads, a choice of puddings and some cheese. Substitute the casserole for a cold dish like Pollo Tonnato (page 67) in hot weather. Use attractive bowls and dishes for the food, and remember, the more informal the better.

Personally, I love weekend entertaining – cooking a couple of dishes in the evenings of the preceding week (and freezing them if necessary). At least one meal should be movable in the summer, in case you want to change it to a picnic. Make Friday supper one which will keep hot without spoiling – for those caught in weekend traffic jams – and the Saturday evening meal a generous roast which can be served cold as Sunday lunch or supper. Aim at planning each meal so that only the vegetables need last-minute attention. We are fortunate to live near several idyllic picnic places, and we like to take advantage of any fine weather. Again, picnic food should be straightforward (a huge home-made pork pie, or a bought one if you have a good enough pork butcher, a generous wedge of farmhouse Cheddar, and of Brie, good bread and butter, a fruit cake, fresh fruit, wine or beer, a thermos flask of black coffee and some special chocolate, like Bendick's Sporting and Military, and a pretty cloth on which to spread the feast) and palatable to all age-groups.

Barbecues are fun if the weather is fine, the food hot and well cooked; this should be obvious, but how often one has suffered half-raw chops, shivering in a stiff breeze, longing to admit that in this country barbecues are not always a practical proposition. If you are determined to succeed, make sure that your barbecue equipment is large enough to cook food for all your guests in one batch, so that no one starves while a second batch is being cooked. Bake potatoes in the oven, wrap them in foil, and keep them warm until needed – or serve pitta bread, also warmed in the oven. Marinate any meat you are using for 24 hours beforehand, to make sure it is tender – use lemon juice, fresh herbs and olive oil for lamb, fish and pork, spiced yoghurt for beef. For real comfort, burn anti-midge candles to stop everyone being bitten to death – another unfortunate feature of evening barbecues.

Business entertaining is often more of a chore than a pleasure. Keep the food expensively simple, so that you have more time to spend on yourself and your table-setting. (This is where the starched napkins and gleaming silver come into play – borrow or even hire what you do not possess.) Consommé and Caviare (page 33), Irish Fillet of Beef (page 52) and Chocolate and Chestnut Meringues (page 97) make a good and fairly impressive menu. Try not to rely on smoked salmon. You do want your executive guest to feel that someone cares for him – he can have smoked salmon in any impersonal hotel.

The most useful form of entertaining is the ubiquitous 'wine and cheese' party. As I do not actually like the combination myself, I choose wine and pâté, or pizza (more suggestions on page 124), keeping the food and drink simple. Wine cup in summer and mulled wine in winter are variations, but hide the bottles of Scotch and gin so that there really are no alternatives which necessitate ice, mixers, lemon, cherries and all the other paraphernalia. Soft drinks should be on hand for teetotallers. Serving the food on large plates on a central table does away with the chore of washing up lots of little dishes with all the glasses; and giving a time limit, such as 6.30 to 8.30, means that you should be able to clear everything away before going to bed, rather than having to leave it to the start of another working day.

FIRST COURSES

One-step soups

Soup is one of the quickest, cheapest and easiest courses to make, and one-step soups are the fastest of them all.

RECIPES

Lettuce Soup

Quick Mushroom Soup

Sweetcorn, Mushroom and Crab Soup

Potato Soup

Chilled Avocado Soup

Celery Soup with Stilton

Cold Beetroot Soup

Watercress and Tomato Soup

Shellfish Chowder

Lettuce Soup

This is one of the nicest summer soups. It is very versatile and can be made well in advance. If you want to serve it hot, use cream instead of the yoghurt.

Preparation time: 10 minutes

Cooking time: 10 minutes

Chilling time: at least 30 minutes

2 lettuces
Approx. 1 pint (600 ml) chicken stock
Salt and freshly ground black pepper
1 tablespoon chopped chives
½ × 5-fl oz (150-ml) carton plain yoghurt

Separate the lettuce leaves, wash and shred them coarsely. Purée the leaves in a blender with a little of the stock, and then make up to 2 pints (a good litre) with more stock. Pour into a saucepan and simmer for 10 minutes.

Remove from the heat and allow to cool. Season with salt and pepper to taste. Chill in the refrigerator until required.

Just before serving, check the soup for seasoning. Stir the chives into the yoghurt and add a spoonful to each bowl of soup.

Quick Mushroom Soup

A quick-to-assemble soup, which can be reheated successfully.

Preparation time: 15–20 minutes

Cooking time: 25 minutes

2 thick slices wholewheat bread
1½ pints (900 ml) chicken stock
12 oz (375 g) mushrooms
2 oz (50 g) butter
1 clove garlic, chopped
Salt and pepper
Freshly grated nutmeg
Soured cream
Chopped parsley

Remove the crusts from the bread and soak the slices in a little of the stock while you prepare the mushrooms. Wash and chop these roughly (if you use a food processor, it will shorten the preparation time by a good 5–10 minutes). Melt the butter in a heavy pan and tip in the mushrooms and garlic. Cook gently until the juices run, then stir in the soaked slices of bread. Pour on the stock and simmer for 15 minutes. Blend the soup, and season to taste with salt, pepper and nutmeg.

Serve hot with a spoonful of soured cream and a sprinkling of chopped parsley.

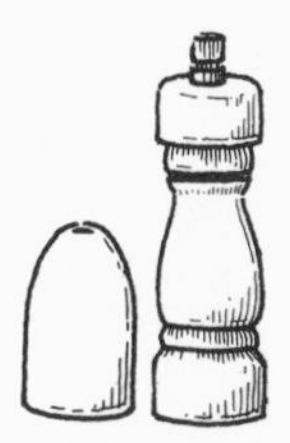

Sweetcorn, Mushroom and Crab Soup

This is a good soup by any standard, and an excellent store-cupboard recipe. You can use fresh mushrooms (double the amount), but strangely enough the flavour is not as good. For a more substantial dish stir in a well-beaten egg just before serving, letting the egg cook in the soup so that it forms white threads.

Preparation time: 10 minutes

Cooking time: 10 minutes

1½ pints (900 ml) chicken stock, made with cubes
1 oz (25 g) dried mushroom pieces
1 × 3½-oz (100-g) can crabmeat
1 × 7-oz (200-g) can sweetcorn
1 tablespoon cornflour
Cold water
1 tablespoon soy sauce
1 tablespoon chopped parsley
Salt

Put the stock and mushroom pieces in a saucepan and heat to just below boiling point. Stir in the crabmeat and sweetcorn (undrained), together with the cornflour blended with a little cold water. Stir well and simmer for 5 minutes. Add the soy sauce, parsley and salt to taste.

Serve at once.

Potato Soup

A good soup for informal entertaining and supper parties. If you can, make it in advance as this allows the flavours to develop.

Preparation time: 25 minutes

Cooking time: about 20 minutes

6 medium potatoes
3 small onions
2 oz (50 g) butter
2 pints (a good litre) chicken or ham stock
Salt and pepper
¼ pint (150 ml) half-cream or single cream mixed with milk
Freshly grated nutmeg
1–2 tablespoons herbs (optional)

Peel and slice the potatoes and onions and put them in a heavy pan with the butter, stock, salt and pepper. Bring to the boil, lower the heat and simmer until the potatoes are soft (about 20 minutes, but it depends on the variety of potato). Liquidise. Add the half-cream, and season to taste with salt, pepper and nutmeg. If you have them, stir in a generous tablespoon of fresh seasonal herbs – parsley, chives, chervil or celery leaves.

Reheat, and serve very hot.

Chilled Avocado Soup

A delicious soup which is ideally suited to being assembled at the last minute. It is important to keep all the ingredients as cold as possible. If you are unable to buy either fresh or pickled chillis, use ½ teaspoon of Tabasco instead.

Preparation time: 10 minutes

3 large over-ripe avocados
2 shallots
2 green chilli peppers (fresh or pickled)
1½ pints (900 ml) milk (from the fridge)
Juice of 1 lemon
Salt

Scoop the flesh from the avocados and put it in the blender with the shallots and the chilli peppers (remove the seeds for a slightly milder flavour), and blend while adding the milk slowly through the hole in the lid. Add the lemon juice and blend again. Add plenty of salt. Return to the fridge briefly before serving.

Serve chilled, with hot pitta bread.

Celery Soup with Stilton

A trouble-free soup to suit all occasions. Danish Blue, Roquefort and Dolcelatte can be used instead of Stilton, but with a slight sacrifice of flavour.

Preparation time: 10 minutes

Cooking time: 45 minutes

2 oz (50 g) butter
1 medium onion, peeled and chopped
10 oz (300 g) celery, chopped
2 small potatoes, peeled and chopped
1½ pints (900 ml) water
Salt and pepper
2 oz (50 g) Stilton

Melt the butter and soften the onion, celery and potato in it for about 10 minutes. Add the water and seasoning and simmer for about 30 minutes until the celery is soft. You can now liquidise the soup, but for the best texture put it through a food-mill.

Reheat the soup and crumble the Stilton into a tureen. Pour the soup over, stir and serve.

Cold Beetroot Soup

Simple but spectacular.

Preparation time: 15 minutes

1 lb (500 g) cooked beetroot
2 tablespoons vinegar (from the pickled cucumbers)
Approx. ¼ pint (150 ml) cold water
Salt and pepper
½ × 5-fl oz (150-ml) carton plain yoghurt
Handful chopped fresh fennel or dill leaves
2 pickled cucumbers to garnish

Put all the ingredients except the yoghurt, herbs and garnish into the blender and blend until fairly smooth; if it is too thick, thin it with a little more water but leave it the consistency of thick vegetable soup. Stir in the yoghurt and herbs. Check the seasoning.

Serve chilled, garnished with a slice or two of pickled cucumber.

Watercress and Tomato Soup

A good soup to make in advance. Add the watercress leaves just before serving. For a more filling winter soup, add 2 peeled and sliced potatoes at the beginning.

Preparation time: 10 minutes

Cooking time: 30 minutes

1 bunch watercress
1 stick celery, chopped
1 medium onion, chopped
1 × 14-oz (400-g) can tomatoes
1 pint (600 ml) water
1 teaspoon sugar
Salt and pepper
½ oz (12 g) butter

Cut the leaves off the watercress and reserve. Put the stalks of the watercress in a pan with the celery, onion, tomatoes, water, sugar, salt and pepper. Bring to the boil then simmer until the celery is soft. Put through a food-mill.

Reheat and check the seasoning. Chop the watercress leaves finely and stir them into the soup, together with the butter. Serve as the butter melts.

Shellfish Chowder

This is a luxurious soup which lends itself to special occasions. Alternatively, serve it as a meal on its own.

Preparation time: 15 minutes

Cooking time: 20 minutes

1 oz (25 g) butter
3 rashers smoked bacon, finely chopped
1 medium onion, peeled and sliced
1 tablespoon flour
½ pint (300 ml) water
2 medium potatoes, peeled and sliced
Salt
1 pint (600 ml) milk, heated almost to boiling
4 oz (100 g) frozen peeled shrimps
4 oz (100 g) frozen shelled cockles
4 oz (100 g) frozen shelled mussels
Salt and pepper
Chopped fresh parsley

Melt the butter in a heavy pan and cook the bacon and onion for about 5 minutes over a medium heat. Remove from the heat and stir in the flour, then blend in the water. Add the potatoes and a little salt and simmer until the potatoes are *just* cooked. Add the milk, then stir in the shellfish. Continue to cook over a *low* heat until the fish has thawed and is hot through. (Boiling will toughen the fish.) Season carefully – you will not need much salt, but add plenty of pepper and a generous amount of parsley.

Serve immediately – very hot, with crusty bread.

FIRST COURSES

Fish, meat and egg dishes

It is very useful to have in your culinary repertoire some first-course dishes that can be made well in advance. Those that need last-minute attention should be followed by a straightforward main course.

RECIPES

Rillettes
Simple Pâté Maison
Pork, Chicken Liver and Spinach Terrine
Creamy Ham Rolls
Eggs with Tuna Stuffing
Raw Smoked Haddock
Scalloped Haddock and Watercress
Mushroom and Prawn Croûtes
Raj Creams
Consommé and Caviare
Cold Omelettes
Omelette, Tomato and French Bean Salad
Oeufs en Cocotte with Garlic Butter
Pipérade
Lebanese Aubergine Salad
Mushroom Paste
Anchoïade
Bagna Cauda with Raw Vegetables
Pears and Cream Cheese
Prosciutto and Pears
Caramelised Grapefruit
Grapefruit and Melon

Rillettes

This may sound a lengthy recipe but each stage is simple and quick and the end result is well worth the effort. Make the rillettes well ahead – they will keep for at least a fortnight in the fridge if they are sealed. Serve with crisp brown toast as a first course or with crackers at a wine and cheese party.

Preparation time: 40 minutes

Cooking time: overnight

2 lbs (1 kg) belly pork
1 teacup water
2 cloves garlic
1 teaspoon each dried thyme and rosemary
Salt and pepper

Remove the rind and any pieces of bone from the pork and cut into small cubes. Put in a shallow ovenproof dish with the water, crushed cloves of garlic, the herbs and plenty of salt and pepper. Mix together well, cover with foil and cook in a low oven (300°F, 150°C, Gas 2) all night (or all day if you prefer). A slow cooker comes in very handy here.

In the morning, tip the pork into a colander over a deep bowl and leave it to drain and cool, reserving the juices. Then chop the meat coarsely with a knife, or by pulling it apart with two forks, or in the food processor. Do not use a blender, as this will make too dense and smooth a paste. Season well, and pack into a very clean jar, attractive enough to appear at table.

Peel the fat from the drained juices. Melt it over a low heat and use it to seal the meat in the jar.*

Store the rillettes in the fridge. Once the seal of fat has been broken you should finish the contents within 48 hours.

* (*Use the drained juices to enrich a stew or soup.*)

Simple Pâté Maison

This is a very good, coarse pâté and it does not take long to prepare, particularly if you use a food processor to mince the meat. It can be made a day or two in advance and kept in the refrigerator. Serve it either as a first course with toast or with salads for a buffet. Pâtés and terrines do not freeze particularly well, as the freezing process reduces the surrounding jelly to an unappetising watery juice.

Preparation time: 10–15 minutes

Cooking time: 2 hours

1½ lbs (750 g) belly pork
4 oz (100 g) pig's liver
2 cloves garlic crushed to a paste with 1 tablespoon salt, 6 black peppercorns and 3 juniper berries
2 tablespoons brandy
1 egg, beaten
4–6 well-shaped bay leaves

Remove the rind and the bone from the pork and reserve the rind. Coarsely mince the pork and the liver. Stir in the garlic paste, then add the brandy and beaten egg. Beat well.

Arrange the bay leaves in a pattern on the bottom of an ovenproof terrine and pile the pâté mixture carefully on top. Smooth the surface and arrange on it the pieces of pork rind with fat side down. Stand the terrine in a baking tin half-filled with hot water. Cook, covered with foil, for 1½ hours at 325°F, 160°C, Gas 3. Uncover and cook for a further 30 minutes, or until the meat has shrunk away from the sides of the terrine. Remove the terrine from the baking tin.

Leave to cool overnight under a light weight. Remove the pâté from the terrine, wrap it in foil and store in the refrigerator for a day or two before eating.

Bring the pâté up to room temperature before serving to improve the flavour.

Pork, Chicken Liver and Spinach Terrine

This is a very attractive-looking terrine. Because of the spinach, it will not keep as well as pure meat pâtés, so eat it within 48 hours. Serve with toast as a first course or with coarse bread and salad.

Preparation time: 45 minutes

Cooking time: 2¼ hours

8 oz (225 g) frozen leaf spinach
1½ lbs (750 g) belly pork
8 oz (225 g) chicken livers
2 cloves garlic crushed with 1½ tablespoons salt and 6 peppercorns
2 tablespoons madeira
Freshly grated nutmeg

Cook the spinach as directed on the packet, then drain it in a colander with a weight on top for 30 minutes. The spinach *must* be properly drained before using, or the terrine will be very sloppy.

Trim and cut the pork into cubes, reserving the rind. Trim the chicken livers. Mince both together coarsely and mix with the chopped spinach. (If you are using a food processor you can put all the ingredients in together and process briefly.) Add the garlic paste and madeira and mix well.

Pack into an ovenproof terrine. Arrange the strips of pork rind on top, fat side down. Stand the terrine in a baking tin half-filled with hot water. Cook, covered with foil, for 1½ hours at 325°F, 160°C, Gas 3. Uncover and cook for a further 45 minutes, or until the meat has shrunk away from the sides of the terrine. Remove from the baking tin.

Leave to cool overnight under a light weight. Remove the pâté from the terrine, wrap in foil and store in the refrigerator for a day or two before eating.

Bring the terrine up to room temperature before serving to improve the flavour.

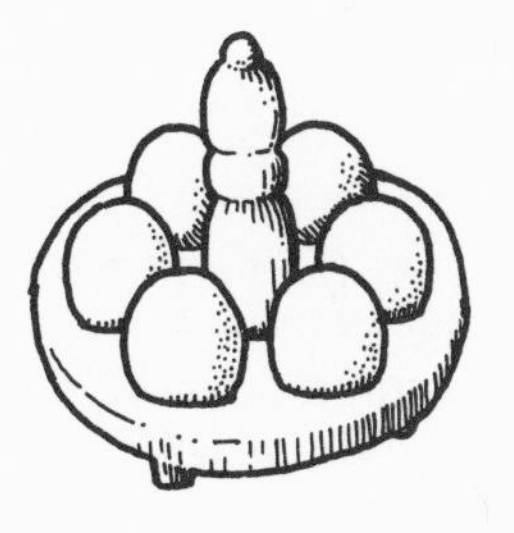

Creamy Ham Rolls

Easy to prepare, and an ideal first course for a dinner party, or as part of a buffet. Buy the best-quality smoked ham you can find.

Preparation time: 15 minutes

Cooking time: 12 minutes

2 large eggs
2–3 tablespoons plain yoghurt
6 oz (175 g) cream cheese
3 spring onions, chopped
2 tablespoons coarse mustard
Salt and pepper
Cayenne pepper
12 thin slices smoked ham
Lettuce or watercress, with oil and lemon dressing

Cover the eggs with cold water, bring to the boil and cook for exactly 12 minutes, then plunge them in cold water to stop them cooking. Do not leave them in the cold water, or cook them too long; if you do you will end up with grey rings round the yolks.

Chop the eggs roughly, then combine them with all the ingredients except the ham and salad. Check the seasoning and spread each slice of ham with the mixture, and roll each one up. Arrange them, join down, on a bed of crisp lettuce or watercress dressed with an oil and lemon dressing.

Serve with brown bread and butter.

Eggs with Tuna Stuffing

The greater part of this recipe can be made up to 24 hours in advance, leaving only the watercress and prawn garnish to be added at the last minute. Stuffed eggs also make a good buffet party dish. Allow three halves per person.

Preparation time: 25 minutes

Cooking time: 12 minutes

6 eggs
2 egg yolks } *or good-quality bought mayonnaise*
¼ pint (150 ml) olive oil }
Juice of ½ lemon }
1 × 3½-oz (100-g) can tuna
½ clove garlic, crushed
Few drops Tabasco
Salt and pepper
1 bunch watercress
4 oz (100 g) frozen prawns, defrosted

Cover the eggs with cold water, bring to the boil and cook for exactly 12 minutes, then plunge them in cold water to stop them cooking. Do not leave them in cold water. Halve the eggs and remove the yolks with care.

Make the mayonnaise according to your usual recipe. To save time, use a blender or food processor – or if you like, use a good-quality bought mayonnaise – this will save about 10 minutes.

Beat the tuna and the yolks from the hard-boiled eggs into the mayonnaise. Add the crushed garlic, Tabasco and salt and pepper to taste. Stuff the egg halves with the mixture, piling it in lightly. Arrange the halves on a bed of watercress and garnish with the prawns.

Serve with brown bread and butter.

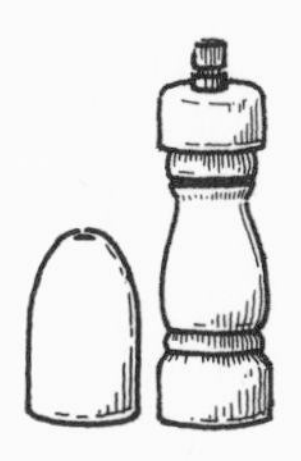

Raw Smoked Haddock

This is just as good a dish as smoked salmon, a good deal cheaper and much more unusual. It is very quick and simple to prepare, but you must use smoked haddock on the bone. Check that the fish is plump and pale in colour, not dry and yellow.

Preparation time: 10 minutes

2 whole Finnan haddock on the bone
Black pepper
Lemon quarters to garnish

Put the haddock flesh side down on a board and press it firmly along the line of the backbone with the heel of your hand. (This helps to loosen the bone.) Turn the fish over and, with the help of a sharp knife, remove the backbone, which should come away very easily. Remove any bits of flesh from the backbone and reserve. Slice the rest of the fish from the skin.

Arrange the fish on individual plates, grind black pepper over the top and garnish with lemon quarters.

Serve with brown bread and butter.

Scalloped Haddock and Watercress

Everything can be done well in advance, leaving only the browning to the last minute – you will have to leave the filled ramekins or scallop shells under the grill at a medium heat to let them heat through before raising the heat to brown the tops.

Preparation time: 20 minutes

Cooking time: 25 minutes

1 lb (500 g) smoked haddock fillets
½ pint (300 ml) milk
1 oz (25 g) butter
1 oz (25 g) flour
Leaves of a bunch of watercress, washed and dried
4 tablespoons thick cream
Salt and pepper
Brown breadcrumbs
Butter

Cover the fish with the milk and cook gently until the fish flakes easily with a knife. Remove the fish and let it cool, reserve the milk.

Melt the butter, stir in the flour, then add the strained milk from the fish, stirring well to make a smooth sauce. Bring to the boil, stirring continuously, then simmer very gently.

Meanwhile, flake the fish, removing any bones and skin, and chop the watercress leaves finely. Stir the fish into the sauce, add the cream, then the watercress, and season to taste.

Butter small ramekin dishes, or, better still, scallop shells, and pour the haddock mixture into them. Scatter breadcrumbs over the top, dot with butter and brown under the grill.

Mushroom and Prawn Croûtes

These croûtes are quite delicious and can be made at the last minute. They do need attention while they cook and are best served before an easy main course.

Preparation time: 15 minutes

Cooking time: 25 minutes

8 slices stale brown bread
1 oz (25 g) butter
2 tablespoons olive oil
6 oz (175 g) mushrooms
½ oz (12 g) butter
¼ pint (150 ml) double cream
4 oz (100 g) frozen prawns, defrosted
Chopped tarragon or chervil
Lemon juice
Salt and black pepper

Either trim the crusts from the bread or cut out large circles of bread with a biscuit cutter. Melt the butter with the olive oil in a frying pan and heat until really hot, then fry the slices of bread on both sides until crisp and golden. Drain the croûtes on kitchen paper, transfer them to a warm serving dish and keep them warm in the oven, with the door ajar, while you cook the mushrooms. (Closing the oven door will make the croûtes go soft.)

Wipe and slice the mushrooms. Add the remaining butter to the frying pan, and gently cook the mushrooms until the juices run. Add the cream, then raise the heat and cook, stirring constantly until the mixture thickens. Lower the heat and add the prawns. Allow the prawns to heat through in the sauce but do not let it boil. Stir in the herbs, lemon juice and salt and pepper.

Arrange the croûtes either on a serving dish or on individual plates and pour some sauce over each one. Serve immediately.

If you have to keep this dish waiting, do not combine the mushroom and prawn mixture with the croûtes until the very last minute.

Raj Creams

These creams can be made 24 hours in advance. Plain poppadoms will do if you cannot find the spiced variety.

Preparation time: 5 minutes

Chilling time: 2–3 hours

1 × 14½-oz (410-g) can consommé
8 oz (225 g) cream cheese
1 clove garlic
1 teaspoon curry powder
Mango chutney
Spiced poppadoms (1 or 2 per person)

Blend the consommé, cream cheese, garlic and curry powder in a blender until you have a smooth cream containing no lumps of garlic. Taste for seasoning, and add more curry powder if you like. Pour into small ramekins and chill in the refrigerator.

Garnish each Raj Cream with a piece of mango from the mango chutney and serve with spiced poppadoms cooked under the grill (see packet for instructions).

Consommé and Caviare

An easy and impressive first course which is most suitable for formal entertaining.

Preparation time: 10 minutes

Chilling time: 1 hour

1 × 14½-oz (410-g) can consommé
1 tablespoon fresh celery or tarragon leaves, chopped
Juice of ½–1 lemon
1 × 5-fl oz (150-ml) carton soured cream
Salt and pepper
1 jar Danish caviare

Turn the consommé into a bowl and, using a fork stir in the chopped herbs and lemon juice to taste. Whip the soured cream until thick and season it with a little salt and pepper. Spoon the consommé into individual ramekins, then pile the soured cream on top.

Chill in the refrigerator for an hour, and sprinkle on the caviare just before serving.

Serve with oatcakes heated in the oven, or Bath Oliver biscuits.

Cold Omelettes

It always surprises me that not more use is made of this delicious, quick and simple dish. By folding these omelettes around any number of fillings you have first courses, lunch and supper dishes or picnic food; by cooking them just a little longer, you can cut them into strips and mix them into salads. The only secret is to make them soon enough before serving to allow them only just enough time to get cold – any longer and they will be leathery. An hour before serving should be long enough. Make one omelette and divide into two, or make them individually.

Preparation time: 5 minutes

Cooking time: 5 minutes

3 eggs per 2 people
Salt and freshly ground black pepper
Butter

Break the eggs into a bowl, add a generous pinch of salt and a good grinding of pepper. Beat the eggs lightly. Heat a small heavy frying pan until really hot, add a very small piece of butter and, as soon as the butter has melted and is sizzling, but before it turns brown, pour in enough of the beaten egg mixture to cover the bottom of the pan. As it cooks, lift the edges and tip the pan so that the raw egg on top runs underneath and cooks. When the eggs have set, but while they are still creamy on top, take the pan off the heat, loosen the omelette and slide it on to a waiting plate.

You can add whatever filling you choose – a slice of smoked salmon or haddock (see page 31), some Boursin cheese softened with a little cream, prosciutto or Westphalian ham, a few shrimps or prawns in an oil and lemon dressing, a little cooked spinach (or, better still, if you have it growing in the garden, a few sorrel leaves cooked quickly in a little butter). Fold the omelette around the filling and arrange on a plate.

If you want to use cold omelette in salads, cook it until the eggs have set completely, and cut into strips when cold.

Omelette, Tomato and French Bean Salad

Cold omelettes are delicious in salads, and they mix particularly well with tomatoes.

Preparation time: 10 minutes

Cooking time: approx. 5 minutes

8 oz (225 g) French beans, fresh or frozen
French dressing (see page 109)
3 large juicy tomatoes
2 × 3-egg omelettes (see page 33)
Tarragon

Cook the beans, leaving them rather underdone, and mix them into the dressing as soon as they have been drained and while they are still warm. Slice the tomatoes and the omelettes, and mix both quickly and lightly into the beans and dressing.

Add the tarragon and serve as soon as the beans are quite cold.

Oeufs en Cocotte with Garlic Butter

The time-honoured way of cooking this dish is in the oven, and this is fine if you have the oven on to cook something else. Even so, opening an oven door is more trouble than lifting the lid off a pan, and eggs in the oven can so easily be forgotten, whereas the jigging of the cocottes in a saucepan constantly reminds you of their presence.

Preparation time: 5–10 minutes

Cooking time: 8–10 minutes

1 clove garlic
3 oz (75 g) butter
1 tablespoon chopped parsley
1 large egg per person
Freshly ground black pepper
Salt

Crush the garlic and work it into a paste with the butter and parsley. Using half the mixture, put a teaspoon in the bottom of each fireproof cocotte or ramekin and arrange these in a large saucepan which will just hold them. Add water to come half-way up the sides of the cocottes and heat until the water is simmering and the butter is melting. Break an egg carefully into each cocotte (it is easier to break it into a cup first), grind a little pepper and sprinkle a little salt on top of each egg. Put the lid on the saucepan and cook gently until the egg-whites are opaque and just set, the yolks still soft.

Remove from the heat immediately the eggs are done and serve at once, with a further lump of the garlic butter melting over the top of each.

Variations are many: try tomato sauce left over from a pasta dish, cream and fresh herbs, even the gravy left over from a stew or roast, or the remains of a ratatouille. For a more substantial lunch version, try mushrooms cooked in a little butter, or some finely-chopped ham mixed with thick cream or béchamel sauce – allow two eggs per person.

Pipérade

Pipérade is an excellent brunch, light lunch or supper dish. For a more substantial meal or for a buffet, turn the Pipérade into a baked flan case and serve cold, garnished with anchovies and black olives.

Preparation time: 5 minutes

Cooking time: 10–15 minutes

1 oz (25 g) butter
1 × 14-oz (400-g) can ratatouille
6 eggs, lightly beaten with salt and pepper
French loaf, warmed in the oven

Melt the butter in a frying pan and add the ratatouille. Heat it gently until it is hot but not boiling. Stir in the beaten eggs and, with a wooden fork, scramble them over a low heat until the mixture is creamy but not sloppy.

Serve at once with warm French bread.

Lebanese Aubergine Salad

An exotic and trouble-free salad that can be cooked well in advance. The actual preparation time is very short. Serve as a starter or as part of a buffet meal.

Preparation time: 15 minutes +1 hour draining time

Cooking time: 10–15 minutes

Standing time: 30 minutes

2 large aubergines
Salt
Olive oil
2 × 5-fl oz (150-ml) cartons plain yoghurt
2 cloves garlic
Salt and pepper
Coriander

Slice the aubergines, sprinkle them with salt and leave to drain in a colander for about an hour.

Heat the olive oil in a frying pan and, while it heats, pat the aubergine slices dry with kitchen paper, then fry them golden in the hot oil; leave them slightly underdone. Arrange the slices, overlapping like scales, on a flat dish and leave to cool. Blend the yoghurt with the garlic, salt and pepper and coriander, and pour over the aubergines.

Leave for at least half an hour in a cool place before serving.

Mushroom Paste

This is a good, cheap first course, and one that takes much less time to prepare if you own a food processor. Make it in advance and serve with hot toast and butter.

Preparation time: 30 minutes

Cooking time: 5–10 minutes

Chilling time: 20 minutes

2 shallots or 1 small onion
½ clove garlic
1 tablespoon olive oil
1 lb (500 g) mushrooms
1 ×5-fl oz (150-ml) carton yoghurt or soured cream
Chopped parsley and chives to taste
Salt and pepper
Approx. 1 tablespoon white wine vinegar

Chop the shallots and garlic as finely as possible and cook them gently in the olive oil. While they are cooking, wipe and chop the mushrooms, equally finely. Add them to the softened shallots and garlic and cook until just soft, then raise the heat to evaporate the juices. Take off the heat and stir in the yoghurt or cream, followed by the herbs, a generous seasoning of salt and pepper and the vinegar.

Turn into a dish and chill until you are ready to serve.

Anchoïade

Serve as a first course or as a light lunch or buffet dish. These quantities would make enough for eight people as a first course, and enough for four as a light lunch. The orange flower water is essential for the flavour of this very ancient (possibly Roman) sauce, and can be bought from dispensing chemists and good herbalists.

Preparation time: 10 minutes

Warming time: 15–20 minutes

2 cans anchovy fillets, drained
1 small onion, chopped
3 dried figs
1 oz (25 g) dates
1 oz (25 g) ground almonds
4 tablespoons olive oil
1 tablespoon orange flower water
2 cloves garlic
1 tablespoon Tabasco
Juice of 1 lemon
1 tablespoon *each* parsley, chives, tarragon and fennel (all fresh if possible)
2 loaves French bread

Using a food processor or liquidiser blend all the ingredients, except the bread, into a not-too-homogeneous purée.

Cut the French bread into slices about 1 inch (2.5 cm) thick and spread each with some of the purée, or *anchoïade*. Arrange the bread on a baking sheet and heat through in a moderate oven, 350°F, 180°C, Gas 4, for about 15–20 minutes and serve.

Bagna Cauda with Raw Vegetables

Bagna Cauda is Sicilian in origin, and makes an unusual and delicious start to an informal supper party. Serve it with crudités and plenty of crusty bread.

Preparation time: 15 minutes

Cooking time: 10 minutes

3 oz (75 g) butter
1 can anchovy fillets, drained and chopped finely
3 tablespoons olive oil
6 cloves garlic, finely chopped
¼ pint (150 ml) single cream
A little salt and pepper
Fresh vegetables in season suitable for serving raw – fennel, celery, carrots, cauliflower, radishes, peppers, French and runner beans, courgettes

Put the butter, anchovies, olive oil, garlic and cream in a small heavy pan and heat gently until the butter has melted, then raise the heat and simmer gently to thicken the cream. Season to taste.

Prepare the vegetables – a combination of three or four is plenty – peeling where necessary, washing them and cutting into strips for dipping. Arrange them on a large flat plate with the *bagna cauda* in a warm bowl in the centre, as a dip.

Provide plenty of crusty fresh bread.

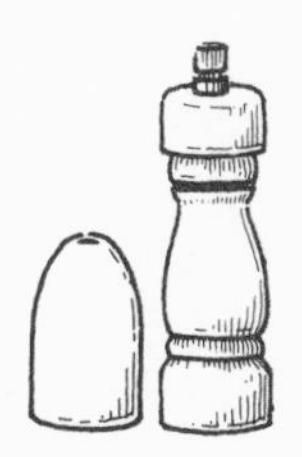

Pears and Cream Cheese

This can be made equally successfully with peaches. The cheese filling can be prepared in advance, but the pear should be peeled and arranged on the plate at the last minute.

Preparation time: 10 minutes

4 oz (100 g) cream cheese
1 tablespoon salt
½ oz (12 g) black peppercorns, crushed
1 well-flavoured, really ripe, large pear per person
½ lemon
Mustard and cress
French dressing (page 109)

Work the cream cheese with the salt and crushed peppercorns. Peel the pears, cut them in quarters lengthways and remove the cores, then wipe the pieces with a cut lemon to prevent them browning. Arrange the cress on four plates, pile mounds of the cream cheese on top and re-form each pear round the cheese.

Serve the dressing in a sauceboat.

Prosciutto and Pears

I make no apologies for including this classic Italian first course. It rarely appears in cookery books but it is the quickest and easiest of dishes to prepare and is perfect for a formal dinner party. Much depends on the quality of the pears, and if you are doubtful about this use slices of honeydew melon or cubes of Ogen melon instead. Even avocado pears work well.

Preparation time: 10 minutes

2 large slices prosciutto or Westphalian ham per person
1 well-flavoured, large, ripe pear per person
½ lemon
Freshly ground black pepper
French dressing made with lemon (page 109)

Arrange the slices of ham on individual plates. Peel, core and slice the pears lengthways and wipe with a cut lemon to prevent discoloration. Place the pear slices around the ham, and grind plenty of black pepper over the top.

Serve the French dressing separately.

Caramelised Grapefruit

This is a variation on the more usual combination of grapefruit and brown sugar – the flavours of the fruit, madeira and caramel are subtle and refreshing.

Preparation time: 15 minutes

Cooking time: 10 minutes

Chilling time: 1 hour

2 grapefruits
4 tablespoons madeira
2 oz (50 g) caster suguar

Halve the grapefruit and cut round each segment with a sharp knife to loosen. Pour a tablespoon of madeira over each half. Put the sugar in a heavy pan, heat it very slowly until it melts, then continue to cook until it turns a rich dark brown. Before it burns, pour a thin film of caramel over each grapefruit half.

Chill for 1 hour before serving in grapefruit glasses.

Grapefruit and Melon

An old favourite – which can be prepared well in advance.

Preparation time: 10 minutes

Chilling time: 30 minutes

2 Ogen melons
2 grapefruits
A little sugar
Freshly ground black pepper
Juice of 2 oranges

Halve the melons, remove the seeds, and fill each half with the peeled and chopped segments of grapefruit. Sprinkle with a little sugar and a grinding of black pepper, and the orange juice.

Chill in the refrigerator before serving.

MAIN COURSES

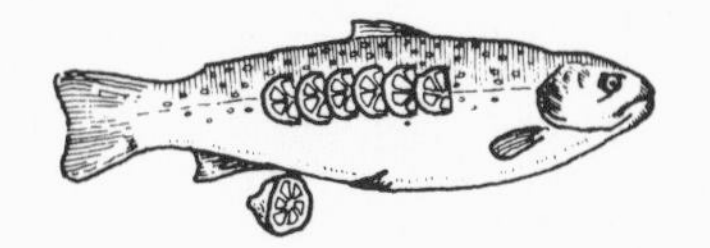

Fish

Fish is often neglected as a main course, perhaps because many fish recipes involve difficult sauces. This is a pity, since fish is enormously versatile and simple to cook.

RECIPES

Fishes and Cream

Gougère of Smoked Haddock

Foil-baked fish

Fish-in-the-Hole with Tomato Sauce

Trout with Shrimp and Chambéry Sauce

Portuguese Fish

Fish Lasagne

Fish Casserole

Seviche

Grilled Mackerel on Fennel

Fishes and Cream

Extravagant, delicious and simple, this recipe also works with humbler fish – lemon sole, plaice or dabs – as long as they are really fresh. Such simplicity does reveal the quality of the materials. Ask the fishmonger to skin the fish and to leave them on the bone.

Preparation time: 10 minutes

Cooking time: 35 minutes

1 oz (25 g) butter, softened slightly
4 fresh sole, skinned but left on the bone
Salt and freshly ground black pepper
Juice of 1 lemon
½ pint (300 ml) double cream
1 oz (25 g) grated Parmesan

Heat the oven to 350°F, 160°C, Gas 3. Spread the softened butter over the bottom of a roasting tin, which should be large enough to take the fish in a single layer. If necessary, use two tins. Season the fish on both sides with salt, pepper and a little lemon juice and place them in the roasting tin. Cover with butter papers to stop them drying out, and cook in the oven for 30 minutes.

Whip the cream until stiff, season with a little salt and pepper and set aside. Preheat the grill to hot.

When the fish are cooked, slide them on to a warmed heatproof serving dish and cover each one with a good layer of whipped cream and sprinkle the top with Parmesan. Place under the grill for a minute until the surface is browned.

Serve at once with a few French beans or some spinach.

Gougère of Smoked Haddock

This is one of my favourite recipes, which can be made well in advance, ready to put into a hot oven 45 minutes before you want to eat. This is a delicious way of glamorising cold chicken, or stretching shellfish – add a few quartered mushrooms, cooked gently in a little butter, to the shellfish sauce.

Preparation time: 30 minutes

Cooking time: 45 minutes

12 oz (375 g) smoked haddock
1 bay leaf
½ pint (300 ml) milk
1½ oz (35 g) butter
1½ oz (35 g) flour
2 tablespoons thick cream
Salt and pepper

Choux paste

5 oz (125 g) plain flour
3 oz (75 g) butter
½ pint (300 ml) water
3 eggs, lightly beaten
Salt and pepper
1 oz (25 g) Parmesan, grated
2 tablespoons dried breadcrumbs
Extra Parmesan, grated

Prepare the filling first. Put the haddock, bay leaf and milk into a pan, bring up to a gentle simmer and cook for about 10 minutes, or until the fish flakes easily. Lift the fish out on to a plate and leave to cool. Strain the milk into a measuring jug and add more milk if necessary to bring it back to half a pint (300 ml). Melt the 1½ oz (35 g) butter in a pan, stir in 1½ oz (35 g) flour, and slowly stir in the hot milk until you have a smooth sauce. Stir it constantly until it comes to the boil, then lower the heat and let it simmer for a few minutes while you deal with the fish.

Remove the bones and any skin, flake the flesh and add it to the sauce. Stir in the cream and season to taste with a little salt and pepper. Set this mixture aside and make the *choux* paste.

To make the paste, first sift the flour on to a sheet of paper. Cut the butter into cubes and put in a pan with the water and bring to the boil. Check that the butter has melted, then draw the pan off the heat and shoot all the flour into the pan, using the paper as a funnel. Beat hard, using electric beaters if you like, until the mixture leaves the sides of the pan clean, then start adding the beaten eggs, about a tablespoonful at a time, with a sprinkling of salt and a grinding of pepper. Beat hard between each addition of eggs, adding the Parmesan at the end. (All this sounds long-drawn-out but is actually quick to do, although it is hard work if you are doing it by hand. If you are using a food processor, tip the mixture into the goblet once you have beaten in the flour, then add the eggs one by one through the tube. There is no need to beat them first.)

Grease an ovenproof dish approx. 8 inches (20 cm) in diameter and 2 inches (5 cm) deep and bank the *choux* mixture round the sides, using the back of a wet spoon. Check the seasoning of the fish filling and spoon it into the centre. At this stage it can be left until you are ready to cook it, leaving the addition of the breadcrumbs and Parmesan on the top until the last minute.

Cook at 400°F, 200°C, Gas 6 for 45 minutes, until the gougère is golden and very puffy.

Serve at once, preferably without potatoes but with a single green vegetable, such as spinach, broccoli, or whole stringless beans.

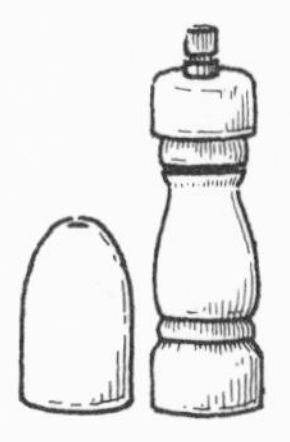

Foil-baked Fish

Foil-baked fish is the perfect way to retain the flavour of really fresh fish, or to add flavour to frozen fish. It is not necessary to defrost frozen fish completely first – the flavour is often better if you do not – but allow an extra 20 minutes' cooking time for a whole or large piece of salmon, 10 minutes for trout or cod and haddock fillets.

Generously butter a large piece of foil. Season the fish inside and out with salt and freshly-ground black pepper, lemon juice and an appropriate fresh herb – either tarragon, fennel, chervil or parsley. Place the fish on the foil and fold the edges of the foil tightly together, but take care not to wrap it too tightly round the fish. Place the parcel on a baking sheet and cook at 325°F, 160°C, Gas 3, for 1 hour for a fish weighing up to 5 lb (2.25 kg) and thereafter add 15 minutes per pound.

Fish-in-the-Hole with Tomato Sauce

This is a down-market version of the Gougère, much appreciated by children. You can use frozen cod or haddock steaks as their uniform thickness makes them very suitable for this dish, and there is no need to thaw them first. The tomato sauce recipe is one of the most useful I know, and worth making in large quantities and freezing. It is excellent with pasta and chicken as well as fish.

Preparation time: 15 minutes

Cooking time: 45–50 minutes

4 cod or haddock steaks
2–3 tablespoons finely chopped parsley mixed with salt and pepper
Lard

Batter
4 oz (100 g) self-raising flour
2 large eggs
½ pint (300 ml) milk
Salt and pepper

Tomato Sauce
1 tablespoon olive oil
1 large onion, sliced
1 clove garlic, sliced
1 × 14-oz (400-g) can tomatoes
1 dessertspoon *each* of brown sugar and wine or cider vinegar
1 teaspoon dried basil or oregano
Salt and pepper

Put all the batter ingredients in the blender and blend for 1 minute. If you can, leave the batter to stand for at least an hour; if not, blend for 2–3 minutes to break down the starch in the flour.

Roll each fish steak in the seasoned parsley.

Heat the oven to 425°F, 220°C, Gas 7. Put a lump of lard in a shallow baking-tin (a Swiss-roll tin is ideal) and put it in the oven to heat until the lard melts and shows a haze. Pour in enough batter to cover the bottom of the tin and return it to the oven for 10–15 minutes to set. Take out and arrange the fish steaks on the batter. Pour the rest of the batter over the top – return the tin swiftly to the oven and cook for a further 30 minutes until the batter is well-risen and golden.

Meanwhile, make the tomato sauce. Heat the oil gently in a large pan and cook the sliced onion and garlic in it until transparent and limp (about 10 minutes). Add the tomatoes, sugar, vinegar, herbs, a little salt and pepper and simmer briskly with the lid off the pan until a good deal of the juice has evaporated. Either stir the sauce hard with a fork to break it down to a rough purée, or put it in the blender. Add extra seasoning if necessary.

Serve the Fish-in-the-Hole as soon as it is cooked, with a simple green vegetable and the tomato sauce.

Trout with Shrimp and Chambéry Sauce

Sainsbury's provide an important ingredient for this dish – their own brand Chambéry, which has a very subtle flavour. It is important to use either clarified butter or a mixture of butter and oil, to minimise the risk of the fish sticking to the pan.

Trout with Shrimp and Chambéry Sauce is a quick dish to prepare, but requires some attention during the cooking period. However, the fish and the sauce can be kept warm for a short time and combined at the last minute.

Preparation time: 5 minutes

Cooking time: 30 minutes

4 fat trout, gutted and with heads and tails removed
Salt and pepper
Sprigs of fresh or dried thyme
Clarified butter or butter with oil

Sauce

¼ pint (150 ml) Chambéry, or other dry white vermouth or martini
½ pint (300 ml) double cream
4 oz (100 g) shrimps
Salt and pepper

Season the trout inside and out, and slip a sprig of thyme inside each. Melt the butter to foaming in a large frying pan and slip in the trout, nose to tail (you may have to use two frying pans). Fry the fish gently for 12 minutes on each side, turning them carefully, using a fish slice in one hand and a spatula in the other. When they are cooked, transfer the trout to a warmed dish and leave them in a warm oven with the door ajar so that they do not lose their crispness.

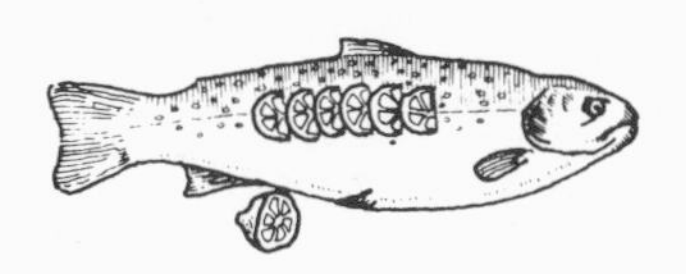

To make the sauce, pour the Chambéry into the frying pan and let it bubble over the heat for a few seconds to release the alcohol. Then add the cream and simmer fast for about 1 minute until the sauce thickens. Turn down the heat and stir in the shrimps. Allow them to heat through, but do not let the sauce boil. Add seasoning and pour the sauce over the waiting trout.

Serve immediately with buttered new potatoes and mange-tout peas.

To clarify butter: In a small, heavy saucepan slowly melt 8 oz (225 g) unsalted butter, over a low heat. Once melted, leave it to stand for 5–10 minutes to allow the sediment to sink to the bottom. Line a small sieve with a piece of muslin wrung out in very hot water, and stand it over a clean 8-oz (225-g) margarine or yoghurt tub. Pour the melted butter through the muslin, taking care not to disturb the sediment. The clarified butter will keep for several weeks in the refrigerator, and is useful for frying and for sealing pastes (see page 111).

Portuguese Fish

This recipe does not need expensive ingredients. It is very good, either hot or cold, and is excellent made in large quantities for a buffet.

Preparation time: about 20 minutes

Cooking time: 20 minutes

1 lb (500 g) white fish fillet, – coley is good
2 pints (1 litre) water, simmered with a bay leaf, parsley stalks, an onion and 2 tablespoons white wine vinegar, 1 teaspoon salt and 6 peppercorns

Tomato and Garlic Sauce

6 cloves garlic, sliced
2 tablespoons olive oil
1 × 14-oz (400-g) can Italian tomatoes
1 large glass white wine
Salt and pepper
1 tablespoon parsley, chopped
Grated rind of ½ lemon
2 tablespoons capers, drained

Make the sauce first by cooking the sliced garlic in the oil over a low heat until it is soft (garlic burns easily). Add the tomatoes and the wine, a little salt and pepper and simmer briskly until the sauce is thicker and reduced. Break it up with a fork – it should not be a smooth sauce – and stir in the chopped parsley, grated lemon rind and capers. Check the seasoning, and cook gently for a further 5 minutes to allow the flavours to blend. Keep the sauce warm, if you are serving the dish hot, while you cook the fish.

Poach the fish in the flavoured water (you can prepare this *court-bouillon* while the sauce cooks) for about 10 minutes at a very gentle simmer. Lift out the cooked fish with a fish-slice, arrange it on a shallow dish, and pour the sauce over it.

Serve with potatoes or rice. If you are serving it cold, it looks extra colourful decorated with more parsley, black olives and lemon quarters.

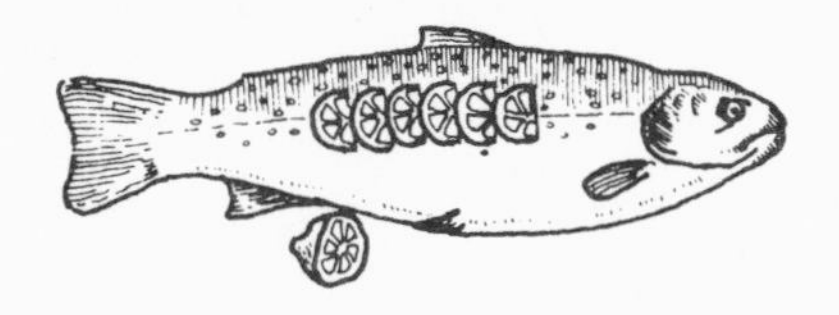

Fish Lasagne

A very useful dish which makes a nice change from the usual meat lasagne. Serve it for an informal supper party, or as part of a buffet menu. It can be made well in advance, leaving only the cooking to do; it can be frozen before cooking too. It isn't necessary to use the 'quick-cook' pasta as my technique works perfectly well with ordinary lasagne. I use the same time-saving method for cooking canneloni, with equal success, and with a quick mental 'thank-you' to the friend who gave me this invaluable tip. Just remember to make the sauces thinner than usual, and layer the ingredients while the sauces are still warm, then add 15–20 minutes on to the cooking time for normal lasagne recipes.

Preparation time: 30 minutes

Cooking time: 15 minutes + 1 hour

8 oz (225 g) coley
8 oz (225 g) smoked haddock
1½ pints (900 ml) milk
2 oz (50 g) butter
2 oz (50 g) flour
1 small carton potted shrimps
2 oz (50 g) mature Cheddar, grated
Salt
Nutmeg
Black pepper
8 oz (225 g) green lasagne

Slice the raw fish, removing any skin and bones as you do so.

Put the milk, butter and flour into a heavy saucepan over a moderate heat. As soon as the butter begins to melt, start to whisk the sauce with a balloon whisk, continuing to do so as the sauce thickens and reaches boiling point. Once it has boiled you can leave it to cook by itself over a low heat for 2–3 minutes, with an occasional stir.

Fold in the fish and cook for another 10 minutes, then gently stir in the shrimps with their surrounding butter, and the cheese. Do not cook any more. Season well, taking the seasoning of the shrimps into account, with a little salt, plenty of fresh grated nutmeg and black pepper. The sauce should be fairly thin, with a pouring consistency; add a little more milk if you feel it is too thick – this is because you are going to use the lasagne without pre-cooking it.

Cover the bottom of your 3–4 pint (1½–2 litre) ovenproof casserole with a good layer of the fish sauce, and cover that with a single layer of the lasagne, without letting it overlap. Continue to layer until both the lasagne and the sauce are used up, finishing with a layer of sauce. Cook for 1 hour (15 minutes longer than normal) at 375°F, 190°C, Gas 5, covering the top with a butter wrapper if it gets too brown.

The recipe for Braised Fennel on page 86 goes well with Fish Lasagne.

Fish Casserole

The vegetable basis of this casserole can be made well in advance, and reheated with the fish for 15 minutes before serving.

Preparation time: 20 minutes

Cooking time: 35 minutes

1 lb (500 g) courgettes
2 large onions
4 cloves garlic
2 large red peppers
2 tablespoons olive oil
1 lb (500 g) coley
1 × 14-oz (400-g) can tomatoes
1 × 3½-oz (100–g) can clam juice, or the same amount of white wine and water mixed
Salt and pepper
8 oz (225 g) frozen prawns

Cut the courgettes into thick slices.

Peel and slice the onions and garlic, de-seed and cut the peppers into strips, then cook these three vegetables gently in the oil until soft. This will take about 10 minutes.

As the vegetables cook, skin the fish fillets and cut the fish into rough cubes, removing any bones.

Add the courgettes to the peppers and onions in the pan and stir well to coat with the oil, then add the tomatoes and the clam juice (or water and white wine, mixed), and a little salt and pepper. Simmer fast for about 10 minutes.

Add the prawns to the vegetables, then the coley and heat through. Bring up to the boil, then take the pan off the heat, cover, and let the fish cook in the heat of the sauce for a further 10 minutes; in this way the fish stays in succulent chunks and doesn't disintegrate.

Serve with plain boiled rice, adding a little saffron if you have it to the cooking water, but no extra vegetables; a salad afterwards is much more suitable.

Seviche

This dish comes from South America and is simply delicious. You do need spanking fresh fish, but if you are doubtful about the freshness of the fish, then it is preferable to use frozen cod, haddock or whiting. The acid from the lemons or limes will 'cook' the fish.

Preparation time: 15 minutes

Chilling time: 24 hours

1½ lbs (750 g) fresh white fish
1 green pepper
1 red pepper
2 green chillis, fresh or pickled
Juice of 2 lemons or 3 limes
Salt
Black pepper
1 heaped tablespoon chopped parsley

Skin the fish, remove any bones and cut into bite-sized cubes or slices. De-seed and slice the peppers finely and de-seed and chop the chillis very finely. Mix all the ingredients together in a large bowl, cover with cling-film and leave for 24 hours either in the refrigerator or a cool larder.

Serve the Seviche with a rice salad and a cucumber and yoghurt salad, or serve it on its own, in smaller quantities, as a first course.

Grilled Mackerel on Fennel

This is a very simple dish to prepare, and the flavour does improve if it can be prepared and left to stand for an hour before cooking. Dried fennel stalks are available from delicatessens and good kitchen shops. Cod steaks can be used instead of mackerel.

Preparation time: 10 minutes

Cooking time: 30 minutes

4 mackerel, gutted, heads and tails removed
Chopped fresh fennel leaves
Salt and pepper
Dried fennel stalks
Olive oil
1 sherry glass anisette liqueur (optional)
2 lemons, quartered to decorate

Make three slashes with a sharp knife on each side of each fish. Stuff the slashes and the bellies of the fish with the seasoned fennel leaves. Arrange the dried fennel stalks in the bottom of the grill pan, put the grill rack on top and oil it with olive oil, then put the mackerel on top. If you can, cover the whole pan with some foil and leave to stand for an hour or so.

Grill the fish for 15 minutes on either side, first under a high heat, then under a moderate one when they are well browned. When the fish are cooked, transfer them to a warmed fireproof gratin dish. Warm the anisette, pour it over the fish and set light to it.

Serve when the flames have died down, with the lemon quarters as the only accompaniment. Vegetables or a salad should be served *after* the fish.

TARD

MAIN COURSES

Meat

One secret of effortless entertaining is to keep your main course simple – choose roasts, casseroles and grills that leave you time and energy to concentrate on more elaborate vegetable dishes. If you are using the oven, use it for everything so that you can avoid bending over steaming saucepans.

RECIPES

Roast Wing of Beef with Yorkshire Pudding

Irish Fillet of Beef

Leg of Lamb with Green Peppercorns

Shoulder of Spring Lamb with Lemon and Herbs

Shoulder of Pork with Fennel Seeds

Pork Chops with Oranges

Fillet of Pork with Mustard and Cream

Gamed Steak

Cassoulet à l'anglaise

Lamb Cutlets Portmanteau'd

Beef and Kidney Stew

Mexican Kidney Ragoût

Stroganoff Salad

Ragoût of Lamb with Turnips

Goulash and Dumplings

Pork and Spinach Moussaka

Stir-fried Spiced Liver

If you live near a reliable butcher who hangs his meat properly, then it is worth paying that bit extra to secure tender and flavoursome meat for a roast. If you are doubtful about whether a joint for roasting has *been hung long enough, buying it about five days in advance and leaving it, loosely wrapped, in the refrigerator is the answer. It will come to no harm – the darkening of the surface is a good sign, not a bad. (Good French butchers sell beef which often has an almost black crust over it. The crust is pared away to leave a deliciously tender joint.) Meat for stews and casseroles can be more casually bought because long, slow cooking will break down the fibres and impart flavour to otherwise characterless cuts. A slow-cooker is a worthwhile investment.*
Steak, and chops are the quickest meals to prepare, though expensive. Care must be taken when buying these cuts, as nothing is more embarrassing than watching your guests trying to chew their way through tough meat. Season the meat on both sides with freshly ground black pepper, but do not add salt until the meat has been well sealed on both sides – salt draws juices out of the meat and leaves it dry. Either grill the meat, or fry it, using a high heat, and allow it to 'rest' a few minutes before serving. The best sauce is made by simply rinsing out the frying or grill pan with a glass of red wine, and scraping up all the pieces left from the cooking. Season and add a knob of butter, then pour over the steak or chops. Savoury butters can be served instead: garlic, curry, parsley or tarragon are all suitable flavours.

Roast Wing Rib of Beef with Yorkshire Pudding

Wing rib is a very good joint – it has all the qualities of sirloin at half its price. This method of cooking the pudding beneath the meat is a particularly simple one, and delicious too. The beef should be medium rare and will serve four people very generously.

Preparation time: 10 minutes

Cooking time: 1¼ hours

3 lb (1.5 kg) wing rib of beef
Freshly-ground black pepper
Beef dripping
A sprig of thyme or rosemary
Salt

Batter

4 oz (100 g) plain flour
Salt and pepper
2 large eggs
½ pint (300 ml) milk

If possible, make the Yorkshire pudding batter an hour in advance and give it time to stand. If this is not possible, give it an extra hard beating.

To make the batter, sift the flour into a deep bowl and season with salt and pepper. Make a well in the middle of the flour and break in the eggs. Using electric beaters, gradually beat in the milk, bringing in the flour from the sides of the bowl and making sure that the eggs are well broken up. When the ingredients have amalgamated, continue to beat until the batter has the consistency of smooth thick cream.

Heat the oven to 400°F, 200°C, Gas 6. Stand the beef on a grid over a baking tin, season with black pepper, smear liberally with dripping and stick the thyme or rosemary on top. Place the meat in the centre of the oven and roast for 30 minutes, basting if you remember. Give the Yorkshire pudding another whisk and pour it into the hot fat which has dripped into the roasting tin underneath the beef. Cook the beef and pudding for another 45 minutes, until the pudding is well-risen and a dark golden brown.

Transfer the beef to a warmed serving dish and sprinkle it with salt. The meat should 'rest' for 5 to 10 minutes so that it is easier to carve. Meanwhile, cut the Yorkshire pudding into squares and pile into a serving dish.

There is no gravy with this method of roasting but a vegetable such as Carrots in Leek Purée (see page 84) will provide some extra juice.

Irish Fillet of Beef

This next recipe calls for the most expensive roasting cut of all – the fillet – but it has absolutely no waste on it and needs little cooking. It is a good dish for formal entertaining or for a special treat. Allow 5 minutes to cook the special gravy, and serve the meat medium rare.

Preparation time: 10 minutes

Cooking time: 50 minutes

3 lbs (1.5 kg) fillet of beef
Black pepper
Good dripping
½ pint (300 ml) cold, strained tea
¼ pint (150 ml) thick cream
2 tablespoons whiskey (Irish, ideally)
Salt and pepper to taste

Heat the oven to 400°F, 200°C, Gas 6. Fold the thin end of the fillet under so that the joint is of uniform thickness. Grind pepper over the meat and smear it well with dripping. (As it is such a lean joint, be generous with the dripping.) Put it in a gratin dish and then into the oven. Roast for 45 minutes, basting about every 15 minutes.

Remove the meat to a warm dish and put it into the switched-off oven with the door open while you make the gravy.

Pour off excess fat and stir the tea into the juices in the roasting pan. Simmer fast to reduce the tea and concentrate the flavour, then add the cream and simmer until thick. Finally add the whiskey and salt, plus a little extra pepper if you feel it necessary. Pour the gravy into a warmed sauce-jug.

Serve with Golden Potatoes (page 89) and a single green vegetable in season.

Leg of Lamb with Green Peppercorns

Leg of lamb can often let you down as a roasting joint, and I prefer shoulder. However, not everyone likes the fattiness of shoulder, so here is a recipe for making a leg of lamb more interesting. Green peppercorns are much more easily available than they were, and you can buy them by post from Culpeper's (see address on page 125).

Preparation time: overnight, or all day

Cooking time: 2 hours

1 clove garlic, crushed
2 tablespoons green peppercorns
2 oz (50 g) butter
1 tablespoon Dijon mustard
3–4 lbs (1.5–2 kg) leg of lamb
Olive oil
A glass of red wine
Cup of hot water
Salt

Work the crushed garlic and peppercorns to a paste with the butter and mustard. Make incisions all over the joint with a sharp pointed knife and insert bits of the peppercorn paste. Cover the joint loosely and leave it to stand overnight, or all day if that suits your timetable better.

To cook the joint, preheat the oven to 400°F, 200°C, Gas 6. Put the joint in a roasting tin on a film of olive oil and roast for 30 minutes. Lower the heat to 350°F, 180°C, Gas 4, and continue to cook for another 1½ hours, basting the meat from time to time with the juices that run from it.

Let the joint sit in the switched-off oven for 10 minutes while you make the gravy. Add a glass of the wine that you are going to drink with the meat, and a cup of hot water, to the juices in the pan. Boil together for a minute or two, then season with salt and a little more mustard, but no extra pepper.

Either Breton Potatoes or Boxty (pages 89 and 91) go well with lamb and will cook lower in the oven for the same length of time. I prefer a salad served afterwards to a vegetable served with it.

Shoulder of Spring Lamb with Lemon and Herbs

This is a marvellous trouble-free recipe. The whole meal is cooked in one roasting bag, with the additional joy of no washing-up.

Preparation time: 15 minutes

Cooking time: 2 hours

1 whole shoulder spring lamb, boned if you prefer
2–3 tablespoons fresh herbs, finely chopped (marjoram, thyme, parsley, tarragon, chives)
Grated rind of ½ lemon
Salt and pepper
1½ lbs (750 g) new potatoes
1 lb (500 g) new carrots
2 oz (50 g) butter
Large roasting bag
Chopped parsley and lemon quarters to garnish

A joint of spring lamb may be wrapped in caul fat by the butcher. If so, unwrap it, roll the meat in the chopped herbs and lemon rind, season with a little salt and pepper, and then wrap the fat round the joint again. If you do not have caul fat, don't worry – just season the joint with the herbs, lemon rind and salt and pepper.

Heat the oven to 375°F, 190°C, Gas 5. (If you are using elderly lamb, heat the oven to 350°F, 180°C, Gas 4 and extend the cooking time by 30 minutes.) While the oven heats, scrape the potatoes and carrots, halving the potatoes if they are large but leaving the young carrots whole.

Put the lamb, potatoes, carrots, salt and butter into the roasting bag and fasten the neck loosely. Place the parcel on a baking sheet and cook in the centre of the oven for 2 hours, lowering the oven temperature to 325°F, 160°C, Gas 3, if the meat seems to be cooking too fast.

Serve the lamb, surrounded by the vegetables, on one dish. Garnish with plenty of fresh parsley and lemon quarters.

Shoulder of Pork with Fennel Seeds

Pork is not always a suitable meat to roast for a dinner party as so many people find it indigestible. It is invaluable for lunch parties and for weekend entertaining, and it is delicious cold for subsequent meals. It benefits from long cooking, so no harm will come to it if it is kept waiting for your guests to arrive. This recipe is particularly good from all these points of view, and it is worth going to a good butcher who will give you the skin and bones from a joint so that you can make the jelly that enhances the cold leftovers.

Preparation time: 10–15 minutes

Cooking time: 3½ hours

4–4½ lbs (2 kg) boned and rolled shoulder pork
1 tablespoon fennel seeds
2 cloves garlic
Salt
Skin and bones from the joint
½ pint (300 ml) light stock, hot
¼ pint (150 ml) white wine
Salt and pepper

As you will be cooking the joint in a low oven, it is better to have the joint without the skin on it; if the butcher has the meat ready prepared, undo the joint when you get home and skin it yourself – an easy job with a sharp knife.

Crush the fennel seeds and garlic with a teaspoon of salt and rub this mixture into the pork fat, poking some of it right inside the joint. Heat the oven to 400°F, 200°C, Gas 6, and roast the joint in a large roasting tin for 30 minutes. Lower the heat to 325°F, 160°C, Gas 3, put the pork bones and skin round the meat in the tin and add the hot stock and white wine. Cover the whole tin with foil and continue to cook for another 3 hours, basting every so often.

Dish the meat on to a warmed meat plate, skim off as much fat from the pan juices as you can, and pour two-thirds of the juices into a basin to reserve for the jelly to use later. Make a gravy from the remaining juices, adding seasoning if necessary, and serve.

To serve the pork cold, slice it thinly and arrange it on a plate surrounded by the chopped jelly – the mild fennel flavour is very good, and a potato salad seasoned with fresh chopped fennel leaves goes perfectly with it.

Pork Chops with Oranges

Although the season for Seville oranges is so short, they freeze perfectly and their bitter aromatic flavour goes very well with pork, and can be used with advantage in any recipe that normally calls for sweet oranges. The lemon juice is simply a compromise.

Preparation time: 10 minutes (12 hours in advance)

Cooking time: 25 minutes

4 thick pork chops
Juice of 3 oranges
Juice of 1 Seville orange or ½ a lemon
2 teaspoons coriander seeds, crushed
Salt and pepper
Oil

Marinate the pork chops in the juice of the 3 oranges and the Seville orange or lemon, to which you have added the crushed coriander.

Reserve the marinade, pat the chops dry on kitchen paper and season them with salt and pepper. Heat a frying pan, then pour the thinnest possible film of oil (corn oil or similar does well for this recipe) over the bottom. Let this get hot, then slide in the chops and brown them well on both sides. Lower the heat and add the marinade juices, cover the frying pan with foil or a large saucepan lid and continue to cook the chops gently until they are tender – about 25 minutes but this depends on the thickness of the chops.

Arrange the chops on a dish and pour the juices over. Serve with a very light Potato Purée (page 90) and spinach, which goes particularly well with the orange gravy.

Fillet of Pork with Mustard and Cream

An ideal dish if you are running short of time – the pork fillet, or tenderloin, and its piquant sauce can be prepared and cooked in less than half an hour.

Preparation time: 5 minutes

Cooking time: 15 minutes

1½ lbs (750 g) fillet of pork
1 oz (25 g) butter
1 tablespoon corn oil
1 glass white wine
2 tablespoons coarse ground mustard
½ pint (300 ml) single cream
Salt and pepper

Cut the pork fillet into ¼ inch (6 mm) slices, and then into 2 inch (5 cm) strips. Heat the butter and oil until hot and fry the strips of pork for 10 minutes, turning frequently. Stir in the wine and mustard and mix thoroughly. Add the cream and cook quickly until the mixture thickens. Season lightly to taste.

Serve on rice, with a simple vegetable such as broccoli or lightly cooked Brussels sprouts.

Gamed Steak

A rich dish which uses inexpensive meat and benefits from long slow cooking.

Preparation time: 20 minutes

Cooking time: 2–3 hours

1½–2 lbs (750 g–1 kg) braising or shoulder steak
8 oz (225 g) streaky bacon rashers
Dripping
1 onion, finely chopped
1 oz (25 g) flour
1 pint (600 ml) hot stock
1 dessertspoon capers, drained
1 tablespoon port
1 teaspoon lemon juice and the grated rind of ½ lemon
1 clove
Black pepper
Salt
2 tablespoons redcurrant jelly

Cut the steak into neat oblong pieces 2 × 3 inches (5 × 7 cms) and roll each up with a rasher of bacon inside. Brown each roll of steak in the hot dripping in a frying pan, then pack the rolls into a casserole.

Brown the chopped onion in a little more dripping (be careful not to let it burn), then stir in the flour and add the hot stock, stirring all the time. Add the drained capers, port, lemon juice and rind, the clove, plenty of black pepper and a little salt, and the redcurrant jelly. Stir well and pour over the meat in the casserole.

Cook in a low oven (300°F, 150°C, Gas 2) until tender – about 2½ hours – or, best of all, cook all night in a slow-cooker, transferring the steak to a fireproof casserole in the morning, ready to reheat in the evening.

Serve with Forcemeat Balls (page 110), baked potatoes, sprouts and more redcurrant jelly.

Cassoulet à l'anglaise

This is not a complicated dish to prepare – it makes a wonderful winter meal. A slow-cooker is ideal, as the cooking should be very slow*. If you are going to reheat the cassoulet, though, be careful not to let it dry out.*

Preparation time: 30 minutes

Cooking time: 5–6 hours

1 lb (500 g) haricot beans
Pinch of bicarbonate of soda
1 lb (500 g) high meat content sausage (Sainsbury's, Marks & Spencer's, or Cumberland sausage)
6 chicken wings
1 lb (500 g) boned fore-end pork, in one piece
Dripping or olive oil
8 small onions
8 cloves garlic
Large *bouquet garni*
8 oz (225 g) garlic sausage, in one piece
Salt and pepper
2 oz (50 g) fresh breadcrumbs mixed with 1 chopped clove garlic, 1 tablespoon finely chopped parsley and 1 strip lemon rind, chopped (optional)

Put the haricot beans in a large pan with a pinch of bicarbonate of soda and cover by about 2 inches (5 cm) with cold water. Bring to the boil and boil hard for 10 minutes, then take off the heat and leave, tightly lidded, for 45 minutes.

This method does away with the need to soak the beans overnight.

As the beans 'cook', brown the sausages, chicken wings and pork in a little dripping or olive oil, then brown the whole peeled onions and garlic cloves.

Drain the beans and put half of them into a deep casserole or slow-cooker, put the browned meats, onions, garlic and *bouquet garni* on top and cover with the rest of the beans. Add boiling water to cover the beans by about 1 inch (2.5 cm), but do not add salt, as this will harden the beans. Cover the casserole tightly and cook very slowly (oven temperature 275°F, 140°C, Gas 1, if you are not using a slow-cooker), for 5–6 hours or overnight.

If you are serving the cassoulet at once, skin and cut the garlic sausage into cubes and add to the pot about 30 minutes before serving, together with plenty of salt and pepper. If you want to reheat it some hours later, add the garlic sausage and seasoning as the cassoulet reheats.

To add extra flavour, if you have time before serving transfer the cassoulet to a deep ovenproof dish and sprinkle the breadcrumb mixture on top. Put under a hot grill until brown and bubbling.

Serve the cassoulet on its own, with a green salad afterwards.

Lamb Cutlets Portmanteau'd

These lamb cutlets are a little fiddly to prepare but they do look spectacular and taste delicious. They can be assembled well in advance and simply baked in the oven for 35 minutes when needed. This is a Victorian Club recipe – hence the rather fanciful name.

Preparation time: 30–35 minutes

Cooking time: 35 minutes

1 small onion
1 clove garlic
1 oz (25 g) butter
8 oz (225 g) mushrooms
Pinch dried thyme
Salt and pepper
12 oz (375 g) frozen puff pastry, thawed
8 lamb cutlets
Beaten egg

Chop the onion and garlic finely and cook them in the butter until soft. Add the mushrooms, finely chopped, and the thyme and cook until the juice runs from the mushrooms, then raise the heat to evaporate the juices as the mushrooms cook. Season with salt and pepper and set aside to cool.

Roll out the pastry thinly and cut into eight 6-inch (15 cm) squares. Trim the cutlets to leave about ½ inch (1 cm) bare bone at the top of each. Put a teaspoon of mushroom purée in the midde of a square of pastry and place a seasoned cutlet on top, diagonally, so that the bare bone extends over the edge of the pastry. Put another teaspoon of purée on top of the cutlet and fold the pastry round, damping the edges with water and pinching the edges so that the cutlet is well sealed into the pastry. Trim off any surplus. Continue with the other seven cutlets and place them, join down, on a greased baking sheet. If you have time, roll out the pastry trimmings and cut leaves from them, sticking them to each portmanteau'd cutlet with the beaten egg.

When you want to cook the cutlets, preheat the oven to 425°F, 210°C, Gas 7, and brush the pastry with beaten egg. Bake for 35 minutes.

Serve very hot, with a green vegetable such as stringless beans. Potatoes aren't really necessary because of the pastry – unless you know your guests' appetites well.

Beef and Kidney Stew

If I have time, I like to make individual Yorkshire puddings and serve the stew ladled into the middle of them, surrounded by buttery parsleyed carrots. Alternatively, serve with curry bread or plain crusty bread. A good dish for a buffet meal.

Preparation time: 20 minutes

Cooking time: 5–6 hours

2 lbs (1 kg) shin beef
8 oz (225 g) ox kidney
Dripping
3 large onions, sliced
2 oz (50 g) flour
½ pint (300 ml) hot brown stock
1 bottle Guinness, or brown ale
1 tablespoon mushroom ketchup
1 tablespoon Worcestershire sauce
2 bay leaves and a sprig of thyme, fresh or dried
Salt and pepper

Cut the beef into large cubes using a razor-sharp knife, without removing any of the gristle which will disintegrate and add to the quality of the gravy. Cut the kidney into smaller pieces, removing any white core. Brown the beef and kidney in the dripping in a frying pan and transfer to a slow-cooker or casserole. Lastly, fry the onions until brown, then stir in the flour, add the hot stock, then the Guinness, mushroom ketchup and Worcestershire sauce, the bay leaves and herbs and a light seasoning of salt and pepper. Put the lid on the slow-cooker or casserole and cook very slowly (275°F, 140°C, Gas 1) until the meat is tender. Check the seasoning before serving.

Mexican Kidney Ragôut

The sauce can be made well in advance, and the kidneys can also be prepared beforehand. The final cooking will then take only 10–15 minutes.

Preparation time: 20 minutes

Cooking time: 25 minutes

2 large onions
2 large cloves garlic
Olive oil
1 × 14-oz (400-g) can tomatoes
Salt and pepper
1 teaspoon Tabasco
1 tablespoon red wine vinegar
2 tablespoons chopped parsley
1½ lbs (750 g) lambs' kidneys

First make the sauce. Peel and finely chop the onions and crush the garlic. Heat 2 tablespoons olive oil in a saucepan, add the onion and garlic and cook slowly until soft. Add the tomatoes and simmer rapidly to reduce the liquid and concentrate the flavour. When most of the juice has evaporated, season the sauce with salt, pepper, Tabasco, vinegar and parsley. Set aside until required.

Halve the kidneys, remove the cores and cut into slices.

Heat a thin film of olive oil in a frying pan and toss the kidney slices in the oil for about 10 minutes. They should be firm and brown on the outside, but still pink inside. Add the tomato sauce and cook for a couple of minutes.

Serve the ragôut on a bed of rice, accompanied by a salad of red and green peppers.

Stroganoff Salad

This is a good recipe for a buffet supper and for formal entertaining, but keep the cooked beef refrigerated in the summer, as underdone beef goes off very quickly. Topside is a good alternative to the more usual fillet as the flavour is better.

Preparation time: 20 minutes

Cooking time: 45 minutes–1 hour

About 2 lbs (1 kg) topside beef, in one piece
Dripping
8 oz (225 g) mushrooms
¼ pint (150 ml) soured cream
¼ pint (150 ml) salad cream (home-made, page 109)
1 bunch spring onions, chopped
Parsley
Salt and pepper
1 bunch watercress

Smother the cut sides of the beef with dripping and put it in a shallow ovenproof dish. Roast in a preheated oven at 375°F, 190°C, Gas 5, for 20 minutes a pound, leaving the beef somewhat underdone. Let the beef get quite cold.

Slice the beef downwards into thick slices (about ¼ inch, 5 mm), trimming off all fat, then cut each slice into strips, ¼ inch × 2 inch (5 mm × 5 cm). Wipe and slice the mushrooms and put them in a mixing bowl with the beef strips. Stir the soured cream into the salad cream, mix with the chopped spring onions and some chopped parsley and seasoning and pour over the beef and mushrooms, tossing all together lightly but thoroughly.

Serve on a bed of watercress, with the Brown Rice, Red Pepper and Onion Salad on page 92.

Ragoût of Lamb with Turnips

This is a meal in itself. If possible, make it 24 hours in advance so that you can lift off the fat before reheating. This is a good way of using those thin, often tough, chops sold by the dozen in supermarkets.

Preparation time: 20 minutes

Cooking time: 1½ hours

2 lbs (1 kg) lamb chops
Dripping
1 lb (500 g) small young turnips
8 new potatoes
4 small onions
1 clove garlic
1–2 oz (25–50 g) flour
1½ pints (900 ml) hot stock
Salt and pepper
Bouquet garni

Trim excess fat from the chops, brown them in a little dripping and put them in a heavy pan. Brown the whole peeled turnips, potatoes, onions and the garlic and add to the chops. Stir enough flour into the dripping in the frying pan to absorb all the fat, then add the stock, stirring until you have a smooth sauce. Pour it over the meat and vegetables, season and add the *bouquet garni*. Cover and simmer very gently for 1¼ hours, until both meat and vegetables are tender.

Skim any surplus fat from the top and serve on hot plates, with a salad to follow.

Goulash and Dumplings

A great favourite. The goulash can be prepared in the morning or the day before, cooked long and slow, and reheated.

Preparation time: 30 minutes

Cooking time: 5–6 hours

2½ lbs (1–1.25 kg) shin beef
Beef dripping
1 tablespoon paprika
2 large onions
1 × 14-oz (400-g) can tomatoes
1½ pints (900 ml) brown stock
1 bay leaf
Salt and pepper
3 red peppers
¼ pint (150 ml) soured cream

Dumplings
3 oz (75 g) self-raising flour
3 oz (75 g) fresh breadcrumbs
3 oz (75 g) suet
Salt and pepper
1 dessertspoon caraway seeds
Water

Cut the beef into cubes, removing the tough outer skin but not the lines of gristle – they will disappear in the cooking. Brown the beef in the hot dripping, and as it browns stir in the paprika so that the meat absorbs the flavour. Then brown the onions and put it all in a deep casserole or slow-cooker. Bring the tomatoes and stock to the boil with the bay leaf and pour over the beef, add salt and pepper and leave to cook very slowly (300°F, 150°C, Gas 2) for 5 or 6 hours.

About 45 minutes before serving, slice the peppers, removing the pith and seeds, and soften in a little dripping, then add them to the goulash and finish cooking.

Make the dumplings by combining the flour, breadcrumbs, suet, salt and pepper and caraway seeds, and adding enough cold water to make a stiff dough. Form the dumpling dough into balls the size of walnuts.

Decant the goulash into a casserole which will go on a hot-plate, and bring it to a fast simmer. Add the dumplings to the simmering goulash, cover, and cook for 25 minutes. If you have time, remove the lid, heat the grill, and brown the top of the dumplings quickly.

Whip the soured cream until stiff and season with salt and pepper and a little more paprika.

Serve the cream separately. Any vegetables should be simple.

Pork and Spinach Moussaka

Moussaka is usually made with courgettes or aubergines, which shortens its season considerably. Try using other seasonal vegetables instead – such as spinach, or cabbage, or simply potatoes – and vary the meat to suit each vegetable. If you have a food processor, it is simple to mince up lamb, pork or chicken to make interesting variations of this very useful dish. Serve moussaka as part of a buffet menu, or for informal entertaining.

Preparation time: 15–20 minutes

Cooking time: 1 hour

8 oz (225 g) frozen leaf spinach
Olive oil
1 dessertspoon coriander crushed
1 lb (500 g) minced pork
1 clove garlic, crushed
1 tablespoon tomato purée
Salt and pepper
¾ pint (450 ml) white sauce, made from ¾ pint (450 ml) milk, 1 oz (25 g) flour and 1 oz (25 g) butter
Salt and pepper
Nutmeg
1 egg
1 oz (25 g) Parmesan, grated

Cook the spinach as directed on the packet, and leave it to drain in a colander with a weighted plate on top to squeeze out all the water.

Cover the bottom of a frying pan with a thin film of olive oil and heat it over a moderate heat. Add the crushed coriander, then the pork, crushed garlic, tomato purée, salt and pepper, stir well and cook for about 5 minutes, or until the meat appears well sealed.

Have ready the white sauce (made by beating together, with a balloon whisk over a heat, the milk, flour and butter until thick and smooth), and warm it gently. Season it with salt and pepper and a grating of nutmeg, and beat in the egg very thoroughly.

Layer the spinach and the pork mixture alternately in a gratin dish and pour the sauce over the top. Sprinkle with the Parmesan and cook in a moderate oven (350°F, 180°C, Gas 4) until brown and bubbling (about 40–45 minutes).

For a more substantial dish, peel and slice 3 medium-sized potatoes, rinse them in cold water, pat them dry and fry for about 5 minutes in a little olive oil. Use these as layers between the pork and spinach.

Stir-fried Spiced Liver

Very quick to make at the last minute for an informal supper.

Preparation time: 10 minutes

Cooking time: 5 minutes

1½ lbs (750 g) best quality lambs' liver
1 teaspoon ground cumin
½ teaspoon ground cinnamon
1 teaspoon ground coriander
Salt and pepper
4 rounds pitta bread
Corn oil
Thinly sliced raw onion
8 lemon quarters
Mixed salad

Cut the liver into slices, trimming away any tubes or skin, then cut into thin strips. Mix with the spices and leave for 5 minutes. Wrap the pitta bread loosely in foil and warm it in a moderate oven.

Heat a heavy frying pan over a high heat and add the thinnest film of corn oil (the sort that comes in a spray bottle is very useful for stir-frying). Add the strips of liver and stir them with a wooden fork as they fry, still over a high heat. Cook just long enough to seal the spices into the liver, leaving the centre of the strips pink and juicy – about 5 minutes at the most.

Stuff the pitta bread with the liver strips and the raw onion and serve at once with the lemon quarters, and a good mixed salad – cos lettuce, avocado, spring onion and tomato wedges in a lemony French dressing.

MAIN COURSES

Poultry and Game

Game is reasonably priced if you are prepared to do the hard work of plucking and drawing yourself, and this extra work is also repaid by the fact that you will know exactly how long the game has hung before you store it in the freezer. It is possible to buy game at markets in the autumn and winter, and a couple of hours spent at a weekend preparing it will give you a supply of delicious and easily cooked food.

RECIPES

Braised Chicken with Livers and Mushrooms

Grilled Chicken Joints with Garlic and Onion Purée

Chicken Saunders

Roast Chicken with Herbed Bread Sauce

Pollo Tonnato e Fagioli

Braised Capon with Celery Sauce

Crisped Turkey

Chinese Roast Duck

Fiery Duck

Pheasant with Apple Purée

Pigeons with Red Cabbage

Corsican Hare

Braised Venison

Rabbit and Pork Casserole

Braised Chicken with Livers and Mushrooms

A very tasty dish which uses chicken livers as well as chicken portions. Prepare the ingredients in advance and cook when required.

Preparation time: 15 minutes

Cooking time: 45 minutes

4–6 large chicken joints
Salt and crushed green peppercorns (see page 52)
8 oz (225 g) mushrooms
Lemon juice
8 oz (225 g) chicken livers
1 oz (25 g) butter
1 tablespoon corn oil
Sprig thyme
4 tablespoons madeira
Salt

Season the chicken joints with salt and crushed green peppercorns and set aside while you prepare the other ingredients.

Wipe and slice the mushrooms and sprinkle with lemon juice, and chop the livers roughly, removing any stringy bits.

Melt the butter in a heavy pan with the oil and brown the chicken joints all over. Remove them to a plate and sauté the livers in the butter until stiff, then return the chicken to the pan and add the thyme, madeira and a good pinch of salt. When the madeira bubbles, cover the pan and cook very gently for 35 minutes, or until the chicken is tender. Cook the mushrooms in a little extra butter and add them to the chicken about 10 minutes before serving. If you find that the chicken joints have not added enough juice of their own, add a little chicken stock (using a cube) to the pan.

Serve this dish with rice and a simple green salad.

Grilled Chicken Joints with Garlic and Onion Purée

This is a very good barbecue dish, and the immense amount of garlic cooks to a mild and delicious flavour. Make the purée in advance, leaving only the chicken to be cooked and the sauce reheated.

Preparation time: 25 minutes

Cooking time: 30 minutes

4–6 large chicken joints
Olive oil
Salt
Purée
2 whole bulbs garlic (red garlic if possible)
1 lb (500 g) Spanish onions
Olive oil
¼ pint (150 ml) chicken stock
Salt and pepper

First make the purée. Peel the garlic and blanch the cloves in boiling water for 5 minutes. Drain. (Red garlic cloves are larger and easier to peel than the usual small white garlic.) Peel and slice the onions. Heat a spoonful or two of olive oil in a frying pan and cook the onion very gently until quite soft, adding the garlic half-way through. Add the stock and reduce to a purée in a blender. Season well and set aside.

To cook the chicken, brush the joints with olive oil, sprinkle them with salt and grill them on both sides under a high heat to seal the meat. Lower the heat to medium to finish the cooking. This will take about 20 minutes altogether. Be particularly careful to check that the meat is cooked through, especially if the joints were frozen.

Pile the pieces of chicken on a warm plate and serve accompanied by pitta bread and a mixed salad.

Reheat the sauce and serve in a jug.

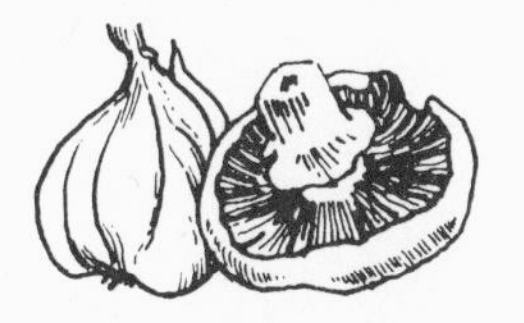

Chicken Saunders

This is a useful recipe for weekend entertaining as you can use leftovers, but it also makes a good hot buffet dish to make in advance and reheat.

Preparation time: 20 minutes

Cooking time: 30 minutes

Just over 1 lb (500 g) boiled potatoes, mashed with butter, milk, seasoning and 2 tablespoons chopped parsley
Half a cold roast chicken
6 oz (175 g) mushrooms
1 oz (25 g) butter
1 oz (25 g) flour
½ pint (300 ml) milk
2–3 oz (50–75 g) mature Cheddar, grated

Line the sides and bottom of an ovenproof dish with the potato. Remove the meat from the chicken, leaving it in fairly large pieces, and arrange it in the potato hollow. Wipe and slice the mushrooms and cook them in the butter until soft, then stir in the flour and add the milk gradually to make a sauce. Off the heat, stir in the grated cheese, using enough to give a good cheese flavour which does not overpower the mushrooms. Pour the sauce over the chicken and bake at 375°F, 190°C, Gas 5, for about 30 minutes until brown and bubbling.

Roast Chicken with Herbed Bread Sauce

I include a recipe for roast chicken because it is one of the most delicious roasts if done with love and care, and one which responds well to interesting vegetables.

Preparation time: 10 minutes

Cooking time: 1 hour 20 minutes

2–3 tablespoons chopped fresh herbs in season – celery leaves, parsley and thyme in winter, tarragon and chervil in summer
1 clove garlic, crushed
Grated rind of ½ lemon
Salt and pepper
3 oz (75 g) butter
3½–4 lbs (1.5–2 kg) fresh chicken, free-range if possible
Salt and pepper

Bread Sauce
½ pint (300 ml) milk
2 tablespoons chopped fresh herbs, as above
6 oz (175 g) fresh white breadcrumbs
¼ pint (150 ml) double cream
Salt and pepper
Grated rind of ½ lemon

Work the herbs, crushed garlic, lemon rind, salt and pepper into the butter. Use half of it to stuff the chicken, and insert the rest between the skin and flesh of the breast and thighs of the bird. Leave to stand while the oven heats to 400°F, 200°C, Gas 6.

Put the chicken on its side in a roasting tin and roast it for 20 minutes, basting once. Turn it on to the other side and cook for another 20 minutes, basting again. Then turn it on its back for another 20 minutes.

Take a tablespoon of breadcrumbs from those for the sauce and season them. Press them all over the chicken's breast, basting with hot butter from the roasting tin, and return to the oven for a final 20 minutes – these will form a crisp golden crust.

While the chicken cooks, make the sauce by heating the milk gently with the herbs for 15 minutes, then stirring in the breadcrumbs and cream and finally the salt, pepper and lemon rind. Cook for a further 10 minutes and keep warm (press a butter wrapper well down over the surface to prevent a skin forming).

As for all roast meat, allow the chicken to 'set' for 10 minutes before carving. Golden Potatoes (page 89) go well with this, and so do baby broad beans.

Pollo Tonnato e Fagioli

This is a wonderful dish for entertaining, as each stage can be done when you have time, none being lengthy in itself, and the whole benefits from being left to stand for a day.

Preparation time: 30 minutes (12 hours ahead)

Cooking time: 1½ hours

1 × 3-lb (1.5-kg) chicken
1 × 7-oz (200-g) can tuna
½ pint (300 ml) water
Large glass white wine
Sliced onion and carrot
Salt and pepper
Bouquet garni

Bean Salad

12 oz (375 g) green flageolet or haricot beans
Water to cover
1 bay leaf
Pinch bicarbonate of soda
French dressing (see page 109)
1 dessertspoon paprika

Cream Dressing

¼ pint (150 ml) home-made mayonnaise (see page 30)
¼ pint (150 ml) single cream
Salt and pepper
Chopped parsley and paprika to garnish

Put the chicken and the other main ingredients in a large saucepan and simmer gently until the chicken is cooked – about 45 minutes to 1 hour. Leave the chicken to cool in the liquid.

To make the Bean Salad, wash the beans and put in a pan with the water, bay leaf and soda, but no salt (the soda softens the beans but salt hardens them). Bring to the boil, then cover and simmer gently until the beans are soft – flageolets will take less time than haricot beans. Drain and while still warm mix with a good French dressing, to which you have added a dessertspoon of paprika.

To assemble the dish, skin and joint the chicken and arrange the joints on top of the beans in a dish which makes a good background to the pale colours of the food.

Lift the lumps of tuna out of the chicken stock with a slotted spoon and put it in the blender with the mayonnaise and cream – if the mixture is too thick (it should pour fairly easily), thin it with a little of the stock. Check the seasoning.

Pour the mayonnaise over the chicken and beans, and garnish with parsley and a sprinkling of paprika.

Serve with a tomato and celery salad.

Braised Capon with Celery Sauce

A capon makes a good dinner-party or weekend dish. It does not need much last-minute attention. Make the stock in advance, and reduce it to half-a-pint by fast boiling.

Preparation time: 20 minutes

Cooking time: 2 hours

6 oz (175 g) unsmoked bacon
1 capon weighing about 6 lbs (2.75 kg)
Salt and pepper
2 oz (50 g) butter
½ pint (300 ml) hot stock (made from the capon giblets and celery leaves), strained
1 head celery
Butter
½ pint (300 ml) béchamel sauce

Cut the bacon into cubes or strips and season the capon inside and out with salt and pepper. In a large pan or casserole that will take the capon, fry the bacon in the butter until it begins to brown, then add the capon and brown it on all sides. Put it breast down and pour the strained hot stock over it. Cover the pan tightly and cook the capon gently either over a low heat, or in the oven heated to 350°F, 180°C, Gas 4, for 2 hours.

As the capon cooks make the celery sauce. Slice the celery and cook it in a little butter over a low heat for about 35–40 minutes until it is tender, adding some stock if it seems too dry, but without making it too sloppy. When the celery is soft, blend it in the liquidiser with the béchamel sauce, and season well. Keep warm while you dish up the capon, and serve it in a sauce-boat.

Serve with Flageolets and Celery (page 87).

Crisped Turkey

Turkeys are invaluable for entertaining large numbers, but they can be dry and boring. Try this recipe adapted from the old method of 'dredging' a bird to keep the juices in.

Preparation time: 5 minutes

Cooking time: about 2½ hours

1 small turkey, 7–8 lbs (3.5–4 kg)
Salt and pepper
Large bunch fresh herbs
6 oz (175 g) softened butter
4 oz (100 g) stale breadcrumbs
2 oz (50 g) grated Parmesan
2 glasses white wine

Season the turkey inside and out and put the bunch of herbs into the cavity. Then smear liberally with the butter, adding a large lump to the herbs inside as well. Roast it at 375°F, 190°C, Gas 5, for about 30 minutes, then turn it on to its side for 20 minutes, then on to its other side for another 20 minutes. This not only ensures that the legs cook as evenly as the rest of the bird, but also revolves the melted butter inside, basting the inside as well as the outside. Finally, leave it on its back and press the breadcrumbs, mixed with the Parmesan, firmly all over the breast and thighs, using a spatula. Baste carefully so as not to dislodge the crumbs and continue to cook for the required time (allow 20 minutes to the pound, plus 20 minutes over).

Dish up carefully without breaking the golden crust that covers the turkey, and use the white wine to make a gravy with the juices in the pan.

Chinese Roast Duck

The flavour of the star-anise is essential to this dish and can be bought from Chinese grocers, or from good herbalists (see page 125).

Preparation time: 5 minutes (12 hours ahead)

Cooking time: 2 hours

8 black peppercorns
2 'stars' of star-anise
4 tablespoons clear honey
2 tablespoons soy sauce
1 × 4–4½-lb (2-kg) oven-ready duck or 2 small ducks
Juice of 1 orange

Crush the peppercorns and the star-anise and mix with the honey and soy sauce. Smear the duck all over with this mixture and leave it overnight, or all day, until you are ready to cook it.

Heat the oven to 375°F, 190°C, Gas 5, and put the duck on its side in a roasting dish. Cook for 40 minutes before turning it on to its other side and cooking for another 40 minutes. Finally, turn it on to its back for the last 40 minutes. Baste the duck from time to time, and allow it to 'set' before carving.

Make the gravy with the pan juices, the orange juice and a little extra soy sauce, adding boiling water to mix.

Serve with brown rice and the Chrysanthemum Salad on page 86.

Fiery Duck

Duck joints now appear alongside chicken joints in good supermarkets and are rather more economical than a whole duck as the proportion of bone to meat is less. This recipe can be put together very quickly.

Preparation time: 10 minutes

Cooking time: 40 minutes

4 duck joints
1 dessertspoon curry paste
1 teaspoon Tabasco
1 tablespoon mushroom ketchup
1 teaspoon English mustard powder
A little salt and pepper
Olive oil

Remove the skin from the joints and set aside. Prick the flesh all over with a fork and work the curry paste, Tabasco, mushroom ketchup, mustard powder and salt and pepper together and smear it over the duck.

Heat the oven to 375°F, 190°C, Gas 5, oil a baking sheet with a film of olive oil, arrange the duck joints on it and cook in the centre of the oven for 40 minutes or until the joints are tender.

At the same time cook the duck skin, cut into strips and spread on another baking sheet, higher up in the oven until crisp.

Serve the duck joints on a bed of rice mixed with fried onion and the crisp duck skin.

Pheasant with Apple Purée

Preparation time: 10 minutes

Cooking time: 20 minutes per pound + 10 minutes

1 large hen pheasant, plucked and drawn
Salt and pepper
4 streaky bacon rashers
4 large Cox's apples
2 large mild onions, sliced
Butter
Small glass white vermouth

Season the pheasant inside and out and wrap in the bacon rashers. Roast at 375°F, 190°C, Gas 5 for the time given above – probably about 50 minutes.

As the bird cooks, prepare the apple purée. If you have a food mill there is no need to peel and core the apples first, simply slice them and cook them and the sliced onions in a little butter and the vermouth until soft. Put the mixture through the food mill on a medium screen, season the purée and serve with the pheasant.

The recipe for Boxty on page 91 goes well with game and is a good foil for the apple purée.

Pigeons with Red Cabbage

This is a recipe for slow-cookers and bottom ovens, as pigeons can be very tough.

Preparation time: 20 minutes

Cooking time: 5–6 hours

1 red cabbage
2 onions
3 Cox's apples
Dripping
2 tablespoons dark brown sugar
Tumbler red wine
Strip orange peel
Salt and pepper
Nutmeg
4 pigeons

Shred the cabbage, removing the central stalk, and peel and slice the onions and apples. Melt a little dripping in a heavy pan over a low heat and stir in the cabbage, onion and apple. Add the sugar, wine, orange peel, salt, pepper and nutmeg and leave to cook down for 15 minutes. Stir well and put half in the slow-cooker. Season the pigeons and brown them in a little more dripping and bed them down on the cabbage, putting the rest of the cabbage on top. Put on the lid and leave overnight on low.

To reheat, decant the cabbage and pigeons into an earthenware casserole and warm in a low oven for about 45 minutes to 1 hour.

Serve with brown rice or a potato purée (see page 90).

Corsican Hare

This is a delicious recipe which makes a bracing change from our heavy English recipes for hare.

Preparation time: 10 minutes + 12 hours marinading

Cooking time: 3 hours

1 hare jointed
Juice of 6 lemons (or juice of 2 plastic lemons)
1 tablespoon olive oil
1 teaspoon dried oregano
Salt and pepper
Olive oil
2 onions, sliced
10 cloves garlic, peeled but left whole
12 juniper berries
Large sprig rosemary
Salt and pepper
¼ pint (150 ml) hot stock
¼ pint (150 ml) red wine

Marinate the hare overnight in the lemon juice, oil, oregano, salt and pepper.

Next day, take the pieces of hare out of the marinade and pat them dry with paper towels. Brown them in hot olive oil, with the onions and garlic, and transfer with the onions and garlic to a casserole or slow-cooker and add the juniper berries, rosemary, salt and pepper, and the heated stock and wine. Cover tightly and cook for 3 hours in a casserole in a low oven (300°F, 150°C, Gas 2), or for 5 hours in a slow-cooker.

Serve with buttered noodles, and follow with a salad.

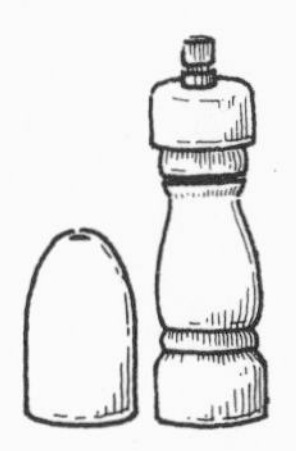

Braised Venison

Venison is becoming more popular and easily available. This recipe is trouble-free and very effective.

Preparation time: 10 minutes

Cooking time: 2 hours

About 3 lbs (1.5 kg) loin of venison
Salt and plenty of pepper
1 tablespoon dark brown sugar
2 tablespoons black syrup
½ pint (300 ml) Guinness
1 tablespoon cornflour

Season the venison with salt and pepper and rub it with brown sugar. Put it into a deep earthenware casserole, warm the syrup and Guinness together and pour over the meat. Fit a double layer of foil under the lid, put in the oven preheated to 325°F, 160°C, Gas 3, and leave it to cook for 2 hours.

Lift out the meat on to a warmed dish and pour the juices into a pan. Slake 1 tablespoon cornflour with a little cold water, pour into the juices and simmer fast until thick. Check the seasoning and serve with the venison.

Serve with Potato and Celeriac Purée (page 90) and Brussels Sprouts with Coarse Mustard (page 83).

Rabbit and Pork Casserole

An interesting combination of meats, which is very simple to make.

Preparation time: 10 minutes + overnight marinading

Cooking time: 2–2½ hours

1½ lbs (750 g) rabbit joints
1 glass white wine
2 sprigs thyme
Salt and pepper
1 lb (500 g) boned pork
Dripping or oil
2 onions, sliced
Hot stock
1 teaspoon paprika

Marinate the rabbit overnight in the wine and thyme and a little salt and pepper.

Cut the pork into small cubes and brown it in a little dripping or oil. Drain the rabbit, reserving the marinade, and put both meats into a casserole. Fry the onions and add the marinade to the onion in the frying pan, then pour both over the meat and add enough hot stock to cover. Stir in a little salt and pepper and a generous teaspoon of paprika and cook gently on top of the stove for about 2 hours, or until both rabbit and pork are tender.

Check the seasoning and serve with floury potatoes boiled in their skins.

MAIN COURSES

Informal Entertaining

The following main course dishes – made with eggs, pasta and rice – are suitable for informal entertaining. They are excellent for picnic lunches, buffet suppers, etc.

RECIPES

George Hardie's Omelette Cake

Spaghetti di Rinforza

Pasta with Tuna

Vermicelli with Cream Cheese and Mushrooms

Tagliatelli with Ham

French Bread Pizza

Risi e Bisi

Salade Niçoise

George Hardie's Omelette Cake

This can be made 24 hours in advance and is very good indeed. Keep it in the refrigerator until needed.

Preparation time: 30 minutes

Cooking time: see recipe

½ pint (300 ml) milk
1½ oz (35 g) butter
1½ oz (35 g) flour
Salt and pepper
Freshly grated nutmeg
8 eggs
4 oz (100 g) cooked, chopped and drained spinach (you can use frozen)
2 large skinned and chopped tomatoes *or* 1 tablespoon tomato purée
Fresh chervil or tarragon
Extra butter

First make a white sauce by putting the milk, butter and flour into a saucepan over a moderate heat, whisking occasionally as the butter melts, then whisking continuously when it has melted until the sauce thickens and boils. Lower the heat and let the sauce simmer for 10 minutes, then season it with salt, pepper and freshly grated nutmeg and let it get cold.

Break 4 eggs into one bowl and beat them lightly with a little salt and pepper, then stir in the spinach. Break the remaining 4 eggs into a second bowl and season, stirring in the tomatoes and a little chopped tarragon or chervil.

Heat a heavy omelette pan and melt a scrap of butter in it. Pour enough of the spinach mixture in to cover the bottom of the pan and fry on both sides, like a Spanish omelette, turning carefully. Slide gently on to a plate and spread with a layer of the sauce.

Next make a tomato omelette in the same way. Put it on top of the first omelette and spread with more sauce. Continue to make alternate spinach and tomato omelettes, layering them with sauce, until the ingredients are all used up, ending with a layer of sauce.

Leave to get quite cold, then garnish with cos lettuce and olives and serve cut in wedges.

Spaghetti di Rinforza

Cold pasta salads can be delicious if two golden rules are followed – allow plenty of sauce or dressing and toss the pasta in it while it is still warm so that it absorbs the flavour.

Preparation time: 10 minutes

Cooking time: about 20 minutes

2 × 14-oz (400-g) cans tomatoes
2 cloves garlic
3 tablespoons olive oil
1 teaspoon dried basil or a generous tablespoon fresh basil
Salt and pepper
1 tablespoon corn oil
12 oz (375 g) spaghetti
6 hard-boiled eggs
4 oz (100 g) black olives

Put the tomatoes, garlic, olive oil, basil and seasoning in the blender and blend until fairly smooth.

Put a large pan of water on the stove, add plenty of salt and the corn oil. When it is boiling vigorously, add the spaghetti, coiling it round as it softens until it is all under water. Bring back to the boil, stir and boil with the lid off for about 15 minutes until tender but not slimy. Drain and run a little cold water over it in the colander to stop it cooking further. Put in a large bowl.

Pour the tomato sauce over the warm spaghetti and mix thoroughly. Allow to cool.

Garnish with the eggs and olives and serve when quite cold.

Pasta with Tuna

A popular pasta salad with children.

Preparation time: 10 minutes

Cooking time: 15–18 minutes

12 oz (375 g) pasta shapes – shells, spirals, etc.
French dressing (page 109) made with lemon juice
Generous handful chopped fresh herbs
Salt, pepper and crushed garlic to taste
Cos lettuce
1 × 7-oz (200-g) can tuna, drained

Cook the pasta shapes in boiling salted water as instructed on the packet, and drain well, stirring as they drain to make sure that water isn't caught in their convolutions. Mix while still warm with lots of dressing and the herbs, seasoning and garlic.

When the pasta is cold, line a bowl with cos lettuce, pile the pasta salad in the centre and garnish with the drained tuna.

Vermicelli with Cream Cheese and Mushrooms

The mushrooms give a lovely nutty texture and flavour to this dish.

Preparation time: 10 minutes

Cooking time: 6 minutes

12 oz (375 g) vermicelli
1 oz (25 g) butter
8 oz (225 g) cream cheese
6 oz (175 g) very fresh button mushrooms
Salt and black pepper
Grated Parmesan

As the vermicelli cooks (6 minutes), melt the butter and the cream cheese over a low heat in a fireproof gratin dish, and wipe and slice the mushrooms.

When the pasta is cooked and drained, mix it into the melted cream cheese and add the raw sliced mushrooms. Season with salt and black pepper and serve. Serve the Parmesan separately.

If you are fortunate enough to be able to buy fresh pasta, then all the cooking times given above can be halved or even quartered. Fresh Parmesan makes all the difference to these dishes and is very well worth the expense. 'Grate' it in the blender or food processor and it will be quite good enough to serve with plain boiled pasta with a knob of butter or a spoonful of good olive oil for an extra-quick meal.

Tagliatelli with Ham

This is very good reheated with breadcrumbs on top.

Preparation time: 25 minutes

Cooking time: 20 minutes

1 oz (25 g) flour
1 oz (25 g) butter
¼ pint (150 ml) single cream
½ pint (300 ml) milk
12 oz (375 g) green tagliatelli
1 tablespoon corn oil
6 oz (175 g) cooked ham
4 oz (100 g) mushrooms
Butter

Make the sauce by the quick method, putting the flour, butter, cream and milk in the pan at the same time and whisking with a balloon whisk over a moderate heat until the sauce is thick.

Cook the tagliatelli in boiling salted water, with a spoonful of corn oil added to stop it sticking, for the time given on the packet. Drain well.

While the pasta is cooking, cut the ham into cubes and stir it into the sauce. Wipe and slice the mushrooms and toss them in a little butter.

Mix the drained tagliatelli, the sauce and the mushrooms quickly and lightly together and serve at once.

French Bread Pizza

Much nicer and very much cheaper than frozen commercial bread pizzas, which make you feel that you are paying for the colour printing of the package rather than for any food inside.

Preparation time: 6 minutes

Cooking time: 35 minutes

2 loaves French bread
Olive oil
¾–1 pint (450–600 ml) tomato sauce (see the recipe for Fish-in-the-Hole on page 42)
1 can drained anchovy fillets
2 oz (50 g) Parmesan, fresh if possible
Black olives

Heat the oven to 375°F, 190°C, Gas 5.

Cut each loaf into three downwards, then each section horizontally to give 12 pieces of bread. Dribble a little olive oil over the surface of each piece of bread and spoon the tomato sauce on top. Arrange an anchovy fillet on each, then sprinkle with Parmesan and put on a baking sheet. Heat in the oven for 35 minutes and garnish each piece with black olives once they have come out of the oven.

Serve hot for Sunday supper, or cold for picnics.

Risi e Bisi

A useful Italian recipe for tired stomachs, and thus invaluable for Christmas entertaining. It really is necessary to have Italian rice for this dish – buy the 'easy-cook' rice available in most supermarkets, checking on the packet that it is a product of Italy rather than of the USA.

Preparation time: 5 minutes

Cooking time: about 20 minutes

About 1½–2 pints (1 litre) hot chicken stock
1 onion, chopped
2 oz (50 g) butter
8 oz (225 g) 'easy-cook' rice (see recipe)
4 oz (100 g) frozen *petits pois*
Tarragon, preferably fresh
Salt and pepper
Parmesan

In a large saucepan cook the onion in the butter until transparent. Stir in the rice and let it absorb the butter for a minute or two, then pour on enough hot stock to cover. Simmer until the stock has been absorbed by the rice and then add another similar amount. Continue to do this until the rice is almost cooked, then stir in the peas and continue to cook by adding stock until the rice is tender but not floury. This dish should be fairly liquid – don't try to produce a dry rice dish.

Stir in the chopped tarragon and seasoning and serve in soup plates, sprinkled with the Parmesan.

Salade Niçoise

Preparation time: 25 minutes

Cooking time: 12 minutes + 12 minutes

4 large fresh eggs
8 oz (225 g) broad beans, shelled (optional)
1 cos lettuce, separated, washed and dried
1 shallot or small onion, thinly sliced
7-oz (200-g) can tuna, drained
1 can anchovy fillets, drained
4 oz (100 g) black olives
Fresh herbs available, chopped
French dressing (page 109)

Cover eggs with cold water, bring to the boil and simmer for 12 minutes. Plunge them into cold water to stop them cooking, then take them out and leave until cool enough to handle. (Don't leave them sitting in the cold water as this helps to form that awful grey ring round the yolks.)

Cook the broad beans until tender in boiling salted water – about 12 minutes. If they are as young and fresh and small as they should be, they can be drained and added to the salad as they are; if not, it is worth spending a peaceful 5 minutes slipping off the tough outer coat.

Quarter the eggs lengthways and arrange the lettuce, shallot, beans, tuna, eggs, anchovy fillets and olives attractively on a flat meat dish. Sprinkle with herbs.

Serve the dressing in a sauce-boat.

VEGETABLES & SIMPLE SALADS

Vegetables can make or break a meal, and one of the surest ways of ruining a simple dinner is to serve too many. Why involve yourself in so much last-minute preparation, and, incidentally, blur flavours, when a single simple vegetable would be enough? Many of the vegetable recipes given in this section are almost meals in themselves.

RECIPES

Jerusalem Artichoke and Potato Ragoût
Broad Bean Salad
Broad Beans with Ham and Chervil
Beetroot in Soured Cream
Sweet and Sour Beetroot
Beetroot and Mushroom Salad
Beetroot and Dill Salad
Broccoli with Bacon Sauce
Broccoli Polonaise
Brussels Sprouts with Coarse Mustard
Spring Cabbage with Mushrooms
Spring Cabbage with Tarragon
Carrots in Leek Purée
Curried Cauliflower
Celeriac Salad with Tomato Mayonnaise
Chicory and Egg Salad
Chrysanthemum Salad
Braised Fennel with Parmesan
Fennel and Ham Salad
Flageolets and Celery
Leeks and Peas
Leeks with Onions and Cream
Leeks Vinaigrette
Breton Potatoes
Golden Potatoes
Devilled Potatoes
Potato Purée
Baked Potatoes à la Ritz
Boxty
Potato and Pepper Galette
Green Peppers Stuffed with Tomatoes and Anchovies
Brown Rice, Red Pepper and Onion Salad
Spinach and Soured Cream
Oriental Spinach
Fenugreek and Avocado Salad
Alfalfa and Carrot Salad
Stir-fried Mushrooms and Mung Bean Shoots

Jerusalem Artichoke and Potato Ragoût

This ragoût can be made in advance and reheated, but it doesn't freeze.

Preparation time: 15 minutes

Cooking time: 25–30 minutes

1 lb (500 g) waxy potatoes, such as Maris Piper
1 lb (500 g) Jerusalem artichokes
1 onion
3 rashers streaky bacon
1 oz (25 g) flour
1 oz (25 g) butter
1 pint (600 ml) hot stock
Salt and pepper
Chopped parsley

Peel or scrape and slice the potatoes and artichokes. Peel and slice the onion and chop the bacon into cubes. Heat the bacon in a good heavy pan until the fat runs, then fry the onion gently for 5 minutes until limp. Stir in the flour and butter, then the hot stock to make a sauce. Bring to the boil, stirring continuously. Add the artichokes and potatoes, salt and pepper and simmer gently for about 20 minutes until both vegetables are tender – stir with a wooden fork if possible, or the potatoes may break up.

Serve with a dusting of parsley, with roasts, or boiled gammon.

Broad Bean Salad

An effective yet simple dish.

Preparation time: 10 minutes

Cooking time: 10 minutes

1½ lbs (750 g) fresh beans (in pod), or 1 lb (500 g) frozen
1 × 5-fl oz (150-ml) carton plain yoghurt
3 tablespoons mayonnaise
1 teaspoon coarse mustard

Shell the beans (if using fresh) and cook in a little salted water for 10 minutes or until just tender – frozen beans and large fresh ones will needs to have the outer skins removed.

Mix the yoghurt, mayonnaise and mustard together and fold the beans into it, adjusting the seasoning if necessary.

For a first course, add 4 oz (100 g) prawns.

Broad Beans with Ham and Chervil

Preparation time: 10 minutes

Cooking time: 15 minutes

1 lb (500 g) beans if fresh, 8 oz (225 g) frozen
¼ pint (150 ml) milk
1 oz (25 g) flour
1 oz (25 g) butter
¼ pint (150 ml) single cream
2 slices lean boiled ham, cut in strips
Salt and pepper
1 tablespoon chopped fresh chervil

Cook the beans as before and drain them. Make a white sauce with the milk, flour and butter (see page 61), let it cook for 5 minutes, then add the beans, cream, ham, pepper and a little salt according to the saltiness of the ham. Add the chervil only just before serving.

This dish can be served with rice as a main course for lunch.

Beetroot in Soured Cream

Beetroot is so often merely doused with malt vinegar, which is a pity as it really is much more versatile than that. You can, of course, buy beetroot ready-cooked, but if I can I prefer to cook my own (40 minutes in the pressure cooker for small to medium sized ones) as the flavour and texture are both better. This is a splendid last-minute vegetable

Preparation time: 5 minutes

Cooking time: 5 minutes

1 lb (500 g) cooked beetroot
1 × 5-fl oz (150-ml) carton soured cream
1 teaspoon cornflour mixed with 1 tablespoon cold water
2 teaspoons caraway seeds (optional)
Salt and pepper

Cut each beetroot into quarters or, if large, into eighths. Put the cream and the blended cornflour into a saucepan and heat through. Fold in the beetroot and add the caraway seeds. Cook on a low heat for 5 minutes, stirring occasionally. Check the seasoning and serve immediately.

Sweet and Sour Beetroot

This recipe falls into the quick-assembly category.

Preparation time: 5 minutes

Cooking time: 10 minutes

1 lb (500 g) cooked beetroot
1 oz (25 g) butter
2 teaspoons freshly crushed coriander
2 tablespoons red wine vinegar
2 tablespoons brown sugar
Juice of 1 orange
1 dessertspoon soy sauce
Salt and pepper

Cut the beetroot into ½-inch (1-cm) cubes. Melt the butter over a low heat and turn the diced beetroot and the crushed coriander in it until the beetroot is warmed through. Add all the other ingredients and cook over a medium heat until the sugar has dissolved and you have a syrup.

Serve hot. Very good with lamb chops, or the duck recipes on page 69.

Beetroot and Mushroom Salad

Preparation time: 5 minutes

1 lb (500 g) cooked beetroot
6 oz (175 g) very fresh button mushrooms
French dressing (page 109)
1 × 5-fl oz (150-ml) carton soured cream
Chopped chives or spring onion tops

Cut the beetroot into slices and then into matchsticks. Wipe and slice the mushrooms, then toss both in the dressing.

Just before serving, pour the soured cream over the top and sprinkle with the chives or spring onion tops.

Beetroot and Dill Salad

Preparation time: 5–10 minutes

1 lb (500 g) cooked beetroot
2 large pickled cucumbers
1 tablespoon chopped fresh dill

Dressing

1 tablespoon vinegar from the cucumbers
4 tablespoons olive oil
Salt and pepper

Slice the beetroot and cucumbers and mix them into the dressing, with the dill.

Chill before serving.

Broccoli with Bacon Sauce

Preparation time: 15 minutes

Cooking time: 10 minutes

2 oz (50 g) streaky bacon
1 small onion
1 lb (500 g) broccoli
¼ pint (150 ml) milk
1 oz (25 g) flour
Pinch curry powder
Salt and pepper

Chop the bacon into small pieces and cook in a small, heavy saucepan over a medium heat until the fat begins to run. Peel and chop the onion, add to the pan and cook until soft.

Meanwhile, cook the broccoli in a little boiling water, uncovered, for about 5 minutes – be careful not to overcook it. Drain well, reserving some of the water for the sauce, and transfer the broccoli to a vegetable dish and keep warm. Make the broccoli water up to ½ pint (300 ml) with milk.

Stir the flour into the bacon and onion mixture, remove from the heat and gradually add the liquid stirring continually. Cook for 3 minutes to make a thick, smooth sauce. Season with a pinch of curry powder, salt and pepper. Pour over the broccoli and serve.

Broccoli Polonaise

An interesting way of dressing up cauliflower and Brussels sprouts as well as broccoli.

Preparation time: 10 minutes

Cooking time: 17 minutes

1 egg
1 lb (500 g) broccoli
2 oz (50 g) butter
1 tablespoon dried breadcrumbs
Salt and pepper
A squeeze of lemon juice

Hard boil the egg for 12 minutes, then chop it finely.

Cook the broccoli as in the preceding recipe. Put it on a warmed vegetable dish and keep it warm while you prepare the garnish.

Melt the butter (use the broccoli saucepan, to save washing-up) until foaming, then stir in the breadcrumbs and chopped egg. Add a sprinkling of salt, a grinding of pepper and a squeeze of lemon juice and pour over the broccoli as the butter begins to brown.

Brussels Sprouts with Coarse Mustard

Particularly good with game. You can use frozen sprouts for this recipe as they are often too spongy in texture to serve whole.

Preparation time: 5 minutes

Cooking time: 10 minutes

1 lb (500 g) prepared sprouts
1 oz (25 g) butter
1 tablespoon coarse mustard of the Meaux variety

Cook the sprouts fast for about 8 minutes in very little water with the lid off the pan – leave them slightly underdone – and drain well in a colander. In the same pan, melt the butter and stir in the mustard. Tip the sprouts back into this mixture and cut them up roughly with two sharp knives.

Leave for a minute or two to absorb the buttery mustardy flavours and then serve.

Spring Cabbage with Mushrooms

This makes an excellent vegetable to serve with good meaty sausages.

Preparation time: 5 minutes

Cooking time: 10 minutes

1 head spring cabbage
6 oz (175 g) mushrooms
1 oz (25 g) butter
Salt and pepper
Lemon juice

Cut the cabbage into strips and wash, then boil fast in a little lightly salted water with the lid off the pan for 3–4 minutes. Keep underdone and drain well.

Wipe and slice the mushrooms and cook quickly in the butter. Stir in the drained cabbage, season and add a generous squeeze of lemon juice.

Serve immediately.

Spring Cabbage with Tarragon

A variation on the previous recipe. The flavours blend wonderfully well, but don't be tempted to use dried tarragon.

Preparation time: 5 minutes

Cooking time: 5–7 minutes

1 head spring cabbage
2 oz (50 g) butter
1 tablespoon chopped fresh tarragon
Salt and pepper

Cook the cabbage as in the previous recipe. As it drains, melt the butter in the saucepan, stir in the tarragon and then toss the cabbage in this. Season to taste with salt and pepper, and serve.

Carrots in Leek Purée

The leek purée can be made well in advance and batches of it are well worth freezing, for use in sauces, soups, or dishes like this one.

Preparation time: 15 minutes

Cooking time: 45 minutes–1 hour

6 leeks
2 oz (59 g) butter
Salt and pepper
1 lb (500 g) small carrots

Slice the leeks into rings and put them in a colander, separating the rings a little. Turn the cold tap full on them for a good minute to wash away any bits of grit and mud. Drain well (in a salad-spinner if you have one).

Melt the butter in a heavy pan over a low heat and stir in the leek rings. Put a lid on the pan and cook slowly for about 15 minutes until the leeks are tender, then put them in the blender and reduce them to a smooth purée. Season. You can add a little water to the leeks as they cook if they are not giving out enough juice of their own.

Scrub the carrots if they are young, peel them thinly if old, and slice them into ¼-inch (5-mm) rings. Stir them into the leek purée, put them in a gratin dish, cover with foil and cook in the oven (if you have it on for another dish) or on top of the stove until the carrots are tender – about 30–45 minutes.

Curried Cauliflower

This is also good hot, using a cream sauce flavoured with curry powder.

Preparation time: 5 minutes

Cooking time: 15–20 minutes

1 medium cauliflower
1 × 5-fl oz (150-ml) carton plain yoghurt
¼ pint (150 ml) salad cream (see page 109)
Scrap garlic, crushed
2 level teaspoons curry powder
Toasted almonds

Cook the cauliflower, whole or in large florets, in lightly salted water for 15 minutes, leaving it underdone. Drain it well.

Mix the yoghurt, salad cream, garlic and curry powder and pour over the lukewarm cauliflower.

Serve cold, garnished with the almonds.

Celeriac Salad with Tomato Mayonnaise

Celeriac is a neglected vegetable, not found often enough in provincial greengrocers. It has the delicious subtle nutty flavour of the tiny piece of root at the base of the heads of celery, now so mercilessly trimmed away by the packers. This is a good vegetable dish for informal entertaining. To save time, use a good bought mayonnaise. You will need a food processor or a mouli-julienne *to shred the celeriac.*

Preparation time: 15 minutes

- 2 egg yolks
- 1 teaspoon wine vinegar
- Salt
- About ½ pint (300 ml) olive oil and sunflower oil mixed
- 1 dessertspoon tomato purée
- Chopped parsley
- Pepper
- Scrap garlic, crushed
- 1 celeriac

First make the mayonnaise – by hand, in a blender or in a food processor, whichever you prefer. (I like to make it by hand, listening to the radio or talking to someone, as it makes a calm peaceful moment in a busy day, but it does take a little longer.) Put the yolks, vinegar and salt in a bowl and add the oil drop by drop, stirring all the time. When it is thick, stir in the tomato purée, 1 tablespoon parsley, pepper and garlic.

Peel the celeriac, cut it into quarters and shred it in a *mouli-julienne* or food processor.

Toss it quickly and lightly into the mayonnaise before it has time to go brown, pile in a dish and dust with more chopped parsley.

You can roast chunks of celeriac (parboiled) round a piece of beef, or cook it with potatoes before reducing them to a purée. The proportions should be 2:1 in favour of potato.

Chicory and Egg Salad

Hard-boiled eggs and chicory go very well together, the blandness of the former acting as a foil for the bitterness of the latter. An alternative method is to pull the leaves from the chicory heads and fill them with a mixture of chopped hard-boiled egg, double cream, salt and pepper and chopped herbs – useful for a buffet as the stuffed leaves can be eaten in the fingers.

Preparation time: 5 minutes

- 3 heads chicory
- 2 hard-boiled eggs
- Chopped chives and parsley
- French dressing (page 109)

Wipe the outside of the chicory heads, then slice into rings about ½ inch (1 cm) thick. Chop the eggs roughly and mix with the herbs and dressing, then fold in the chicory rings only just before serving.

Chrysanthemum Salad

This may sound Japanese, but it is in fact an Italian recipe and surprisingly good – the petals having a bitter flavour not unlike chicory. You need the great big tightly-packed blooms, which never seem to respond to arrangement in vases anyway.

Preparation time: 2 minutes

2 heads yellow chrysanthemums, rinsed
Dressing
1 tablespoon lemon juice
5 tablespoons olive oil
Salt

Make the dressing by mixing together the three ingredients in the bottom of a glass bowl. Arrange the salad servers in the bowl at right angles to each other across the dressing. Pull the petals from the flowers and pile them lightly on top of the servers, which will stop them falling into the dressing.

Mix all together only at the last minute.

Braised Fennel with Parmesan

A good dish for a formal dinner.

Preparation time: 5 minutes

Cooking time: 20–25 minutes

2 large heads of fennel
½ oz (12 g) butter
Salt and pepper
Sherry glass white wine
1 oz (25 g) grated Parmesan, fresh if possible

Remove any bits of the outer layer of the fennel if they look tough, then cut each head into quarters. Melt the butter in a heavy shallow pan which will hold the fennel in one layer. Turn the fennel in the melted butter so that all sides are buttery, season lightly, pour in the wine and cover with a lid (of foil, if the pan doesn't have its own). Cook gently for 15–20 minutes until tender, basting every so often.

Transfer to a heatproof serving dish if necessary. Sprinkle with the Parmesan and brown for a few minutes under the grill.

Fennel and Ham Salad

A very good accompaniment to cold chicken.

Preparation time: 5 minutes

1 thick slice boiled ham
1 large head of fennel
1 shallot or small onion, finely chopped
French dressing made with lemon juice (page 109)
Chopped fennel leaves, to garnish

Cut the ham into cubes and the fennel into thin slices. Stir the shallot or onion into the dressing and mix with the ham and fennel. Scatter with the chopped fennel leaves.

Flageolets are those green haricot beans to be found in more sophisticated health-food shops. They do not keep for ever, their best season being from October to May when they are fresh. They do not need soaking first, and their flavour is far superior to that of the dried haricots.

Flageolets and Celery

A good accompaniment to anything from sausages to stew, and one which can be cooked in advance and reheated (but do not freeze). Flageolets cooked in this way (but without the celery) make a good salad, with plenty of French dressing mixed with them while they are still warm. Add chopped raw onion, black olives and drained tuna for a buffet salad.

Preparation time: 5 minutes

Cooking time: 45 minutes–1 hour

8 oz (225 g) flageolets
Bouquet garni
6 sticks celery
2 oz (50 g) butter
Salt and pepper
Chopped celery leaves

Put the flageolets into a pan with the *bouquet garni*, cover with cold water by at least 2 inches (5 cm), but do not add any salt. Bring to the boil, then simmer for about 45 minutes–1 hour until the beans are tender but not broken.

As the beans cook, slice the celery into ½-inch (1-cm) thick rings, and braise in the butter with salt and pepper for 30 minutes.

Drain the flageolets and mix with the braised celery. Keep warm. Stir in the chopped celery leaves just before serving, together with more salt if necessary.

Leeks and Peas

Any left over will turn into a delicious soup.

Preparation time: 5 minutes

Cooking time: 15–20 minutes

1 lb (500 g) trimmed leeks
2 oz (50 g) butter
Salt and pepper
8 oz (225 g) frozen *petits pois*
¼ pint (150 ml) double cream
Nutmeg

Cut the leeks into thick rings and wash them thoroughly under running water. Drain well.

Melt the butter in a heavy pan and add the drained leeks, season lightly, mix well and cook, covered, over a medium heat for about 15 minutes. When they are almost done, add the frozen peas to the pan, raising the heat as you do so. Cook the peas for 5 minutes, then add the cream and cook fast until the cream thickens. Season with salt, pepper and nutmeg.

Leeks with Onions and Cream

A variation, using onions instead of peas.

Preparation time: 5 minutes

Cooking time: 15–20 minutes

Ingredients as for previous recipe, but substitute 8 oz (225 g) frozen button onions for the peas.

Cook in the same way as the preceding recipe, but add the onions a good 10 minutes before the leeks are done, and season the finished dish more highly with nutmeg.

Leeks Vinaigrette

The best leeks to use for this recipe are those that are no thicker than a pencil, which are usually only obtainable if you grow them yourself.

Preparation time: 5–10 minutes

Cooking time: 5–10 minutes

1 lb (500 g) trimmed leeks
French dressing (page 109)
2 teaspoons Dijon mustard
½ small onion, finely chopped
Finely chopped parsley

If you are having to use shop-bought leeks, halve or quarter them lengthways, removing any tough outer layers, and cook for only 5 minutes in the least possible amount of water. Cook the thin leeks whole for 10 minutes. Drain well. Mix the dressing with the mustard and onion and pour over the leeks while they are still warm. Sprinkle with finely chopped parsley, and serve cold.

If we chose varieties of potatoes with as much care as we choose apples, we would not be fobbed off with watery tasteless tubers simply sold, unhelpfully, as 'Whites' or 'Reds'. Thank goodness for Marks and Spencer and Sainsbury who now sell named potatoes – of these Maris Piper is the nicest and most useful. It is floury enough to produce good baked, boiled, mashed and roast potatoes, but just solid enough not to disintegrate too much in salads. If you can grow your own, try a Continental variety such as Aura or Kipfler, deliciously flavoured, with waxy yellow flesh.

Breton Potatoes

Preparation time: 10 minutes

Cooking time: 20 minutes

1 lb (500 g) Maris Piper potatoes
1 large onion
2 large peeled tomatoes, or a small can of tomatoes
2 cloves garlic
Hot stock
Salt and pepper

Peel the potatoes and cut them into ¾-inch (2-cm) cubes. Chop the onion, slice the tomatoes, crush the garlic lightly and put all in a heavy casserole. Add hot stock to cover, and add a little salt and pepper. Simmer gently for about 20 minutes, raising the heat to evaporate excess liquid, but being careful not to let the potatoes burn.

Golden Potatoes

Preparation time: 5 minutes

Cooking time: 30 minutes

1½ lbs (750 g) small potatoes, fairly uniform in size
Olive oil
Salt
Chopped parsley

Scrub the potatoes and boil them for 15 minutes in salted water. Drain well.

Heat a large heavy frying pan, then pour in about ¼ inch (5 mm) olive oil, heat for another few seconds, then tip in the potatoes carefully. Lower the heat to medium and continue to cook the potatoes for about 15 minutes, turning them every so often, until the centres are soft and the skins crisp and gold.

Lift them into a warmed dish with a slotted spoon, and scatter with salt and chopped parsley before serving.

Devilled Potatoes

Preparation time: 10 minutes

Cooking time: 20–25 minutes

1 lb (500 g) new potatoes
1 oz (25 g) butter
1 teaspoon curry paste
1 tablespoon wine vinegar
Pinch salt
Pinch cayenne

Scrape and boil the potatoes in salted water for about 20 minutes. Drain.

Melt the butter in the pan and stir in the seasonings. Stir the potatoes round in the devil mixture so that they absorb the butter.

Potato Purée

Peel the potatoes, cut them into large cubes and cook them for 15–20 minutes in just enough water to cover – don't drown them. When they are done, pour off the water and return the potatoes to a low heat to dry out. Pour a generous amount of creamy milk into the pan to warm with the potatoes, then beat to a purée with an electric whisk, adding lots of butter, freshly-ground pepper and nutmeg. Serve piled lightly in a dish.

To vary the flavours, cook different root vegetables with the potatoes. I have already mentioned celeriac, but try small amounts of swede, or parsnip, or carrot, or turnip – always in the proportion of 2 parts potato to 1 of the other vegetable.

Baked Potatoes à la Ritz

This is a wonderful supper dish to serve after the cinema, if you have an automatic oven timer.

Preparation time: 5 minutes

Cooking time: 1 hour

4 large Maris Piper potatoes, scrubbed
2 jars Danish caviare
4 oz (100 g) unsalted butter
¼ pint (150 ml) thick cream
Salt and pepper

Put a skewer through each potato (or stick them on a spike-murphy), then bake them for about 1 hour at 375°F, 190°C, Gas 5 until soft.

Stand each potato in a mug or cup to keep it upright and cut the top off, like a boiled egg. Put the mugs containing the potatoes on 4 large plates, put some of the butter and caviare on the side of each plate, the cream in a jug, and salt and pepper available, so that everyone can add as much as they like of each to the floury inside of the potato. Eat with a teaspoon.

Boxty

You can also cook Boxty in a frying pan on top of the stove, turning it over half-way through by inverting it on to a plate, adding a little extra dripping to the pan, and returning it to the pan raw side down. Cooked in the oven, this is a trouble-free way of serving potatoes.

Preparation time: 10–15 minutes

Cooking time: about 35 minutes

1 lb (500 g) potatoes
6 oz (175 g) plain flour
Salt and pepper
Milk
Dripping

Heat the oven to 400°F, 200°C, Gas 6.

Peel the potatoes and grate them (or chop them, not too finely, in a food processor). Mix well with the flour, salt and pepper, and add enough milk to make a thick batter.

Heat 1 tablespoon dripping in a baking tin until a haze rises from it, and pour in the potato batter. Cook in the oven for about 30 minutes, until golden.

Potato and Pepper Galette

Very good with Goulash, or the Rabbit and Pork Casserole on page 72.

Preparation time: 15 minutes

Cooking time: 25–30 minutes

1 lb (500 g) potatoes
1 green pepper
1 red pepper
2 tablespoons butter and oil mixed
1 clove garlic
Salt

Peel the potatoes and cut them into matchsticks either by hand or by using the *mouli-julienne* or a food processor. Put the matchsticks in a colander and rinse them in cold water, then pat dry in a tea-cloth. De-seed the peppers, chop them finely and mix with the potatoes.

Heat 2 tablespoons butter and oil in a heavy frying pan and tip in the peppers and potatoes. Flatten them in an even layer over the bottom of the pan. Crush the garlic with salt and sprinkle it over the potatoes. Cover the pan with a lid, or foil, and cook gently for 15 minutes.

Invert the galette on to a plate, heat a little more butter and oil in the frying pan and slide the galette back, raw side down. Continue to cook, covered, for another 10 minutes or so, until the potatoes are cooked through.

Green Peppers Stuffed with Tomatoes and Anchovies

These may be served hot with roasts, or as a first course. Cold, they make a delicious salad with seasoned yoghurt poured over them.

Preparation time: 15–20 minutes

Cooking time: 40 minutes

3 large tomatoes
1 can anchovy fillets
2 oz (50 g) brown breadcrumbs (wholemeal bread for preference)
1 clove garlic, crushed
Salt and pepper
4 green peppers
Olive oil

Peel the tomatoes by pouring boiling water over them and leaving them for a minute or two until the skin splits. Chop them roughly.

Drain and chop the anchovies, and mix them with the breadcrumbs, tomatoes, the crushed garlic, a little salt and plenty of pepper.

Halve and de-seed the peppers, then blanch them for 5 minutes in boiling, salted water. Drain well, then stuff with the tomato mixture. Dribble a little oil over the top of each, and oil the container you are cooking them in (a shallow ovenproof dish in which they can be served is best). Cook for 40 minutes at 350°F, 180°C, Gas 4.

Brown Rice, Red Pepper and Onion Salad

A good buffet salad – be generous with the dressing.

Preparation time: 10 minutes

Cooking time: 35–40 minutes

8 oz (225 g) brown rice
Double quantity French dressing (page 109)
2 large red peppers
1 mild onion

Cook the brown rice in simmering salted water for about 35–40 minutes – it takes much longer than ordinary rice. Drain well in a colander, then return it to the pan over a gentle heat for another minute to dry out. Mix with the dressing while still warm.

When cold, add the red pepper cut in strips, and the onion finely sliced.

Spinach and Soured Cream

Very good with devilled dishes.

Preparation time: 5 minutes

Cooking time: 10 minutes

8 oz (225 g) frozen leaf spinach
1 × 5-fl oz (150-ml) carton soured cream
1 teaspoon ground cumin
Scrap garlic
Salt and pepper

Cook the spinach as directed on the packet, drain in a colander with a weighted plate on top. The further ahead you can do this the better.

Chop the spinach roughly and reheat in the soured cream, seasoning with the cumin, garlic, salt and pepper.

Oriental Spinach

Good enough to serve on its own as a first course.

Preparation time: 10 minutes

Cooking time: 10 minutes

1 oz (25 g) raisins or sultanas
8 oz (225 g) frozen spinach
1 teaspoon ground cinnamon
Pinch ground ginger
½ oz (12 g) butter
1 oz (25 g) almonds, blanched and chopped
Salt
Freshly ground black pepper

Pour boiling water over the raisins or sultanas and leave them to soak while you cook and drain the spinach, as directed on the packet.

Heat the spices in the butter over a medium heat, add the almonds and cook until light brown. They burn easily, so stir frequently. Add the drained spinach and drained raisins and toss together until heated through. Check the seasoning, and add salt and plenty of ground black pepper to taste.

Shoots and sprouts grown in jars in the kitchen are very useful for varying salads; they are labour-saving to use as they need little or no preparation. The seeds are widely available in garden centres and health-food shops, and directions for growing them can be found on the packets.

Fenugreek and Avocado Salad

The crisp texture of the fenugreek shoots contrasts pleasantly with the creaminess of the avocado.

Preparation time: 5 minutes

2 ripe avocado pears
French dressing made with lemon juice (see page 109)
1 jar fenugreek shoots
Pinch powdered fenugreek

Peel and slice the avocados and toss the slices quickly in the dressing before they can discolour. Fold in the shoots quickly and lightly and add a little powdered fenugreek to accentuate the spicy flavour.

Alfalfa and Carrot Salad

Preparation time: 10 minutes

3 carrots
A large handful of alfalfa shoots
French dressing made with lemon juice (page 109)
1 × 5-fl oz (150-ml) carton plain yoghurt
1 clove garlic, crushed

Peel and shred the carrots and mix them with all the other ingredients.

Stir-fried Mushrooms and Mung Bean Shoots

An ideal vegetable dish to prepare at the last minute.

Preparation time: 5 minutes

Cooking time: 2–3 minutes

1 tablespoon sunflower oil
8 oz (225 g) very fresh button mushrooms, finely sliced
4 oz (100 g) bean sprouts
Salt and pepper
1 tablespoon soy sauce

Heat a heavy frying pan, then add the oil and heat for another minute. Have ready the sliced mushrooms and add them with the bean shoots to the pan, stirring continuously as they cook – only 2–3 minutes to heat them through. Season with salt and pepper and soy sauce and serve immediately.

DESSERTS & PUDDINGS

Although it was once customary to serve two desserts at a dinner party (and still is in many parts of the country, presenting delicious dilemmas), one is really plenty, and always appreciated, even by cheese-and-fruit afficionados. *They are invaluable in areas where it is difficult to rely on a good supply of cheese.*

RECIPES

Kiss-me-quick Pudding
Coffee and Marsala Cake
Chocolate and Chestnut Meringues
Frankie's Sugared Avocados
Basic Pancakes
Pancakes with Brandy Butter
Pancakes with Raspberry Butter
Autumn Pudding
Angel Cake with Blackcurrant Purée
Cherryfield Tartlets
Dried Apricot Fool
Dried Fruit Salad
Rhubarb Glory
Orange Trifle
Strawberries and Chambéry
Cream Cheese and Fresh Pineapple
Lemon Creams
Raspberry Sorbet
Eton Mess Ice-cream
Orange and Lemon Ice-cream
Fresh Peach Melba
Yoghurt Syllabub
Yoghurt Fruit Salad
Iced Cheese

Kiss-me-quick Pudding

There is nowadays a refined reluctance to eat – or make – puddings. Apart from the fact that slimming is fashionable, few of us do the sort of hard outdoor work that creates an appetite for suet puddings. A steamed sponge pudding, however, is quick to assemble and very light. It can be left to cook by itself while the rest of the meal is attended to. And it is surprising how quickly the slimmers and the office-bound change their minds when faced with one.

Preparation time: 10 minutes

Cooking time: 1½ hours

4 oz (100 g) soft margarine
4 oz (100 g) caster sugar
6 oz (175 g) self-raising flour
2 oz (50 g) ground almonds
2 eggs
½ teaspoon almond essence
Pinch salt
½ pint (300 ml) whipping cream, chilled
2 teaspoons caster sugar
1–2 teaspoons triple-strength orange flower water or rose water (available from chemists)
Icing sugar

Grease a 2-pint (1-litre) pudding basin.

Put the margarine, caster sugar, flour, ground almonds, eggs, almond essence and salt into a bowl and beat hard for 1 minute. Spoon this mixture into the greased basin and cover with a butter wrapper, then tie a large clean handkerchief over the top of the basin with string, knotting the corners of the handkerchief together to make a handle for lifting the basin.

Put the basin in a large saucepan and put in enough boiling water to come half-way up the sides of the basin. Cover the pan and simmer for 1½ hours, topping up the water if necessary. (A well-fitting lid on your saucepan will prevent the water from evaporating quickly.)

Before serving, whip the chilled cream in a cold bowl with chilled beaters, and fold in the sugar and rose or orange flower water to taste. Keep the cream cool until required.

Turn the pudding on to a warmed plate, dust with icing sugar and serve immediately. Serve the whipped cream in a separate bowl.

Coffee and Marsala Cake

This is a very obliging dessert – trouble-free and should be made well in advance. It is easy to think of variations on the same theme: a lemon sponge with an orange and Cointreau syrup, chocolate with coffee and brandy, or even a plain sponge with a Kirsch syrup.

Preparation time: 20 minutes

Cooking time: 35 minutes

6 oz (175 g) soft margarine
6 oz (175 g) caster sugar
2 large eggs
6 oz (175 g) self-raising flour
1 tablespoon instant coffee dissolved in 1 tablespoon hot water
Pinch salt

Syrup
4 oz (100 g) brown sugar
¼ pint (150 ml) strong black coffee
3 tablespoons marsala

½ pint (300 ml) whipped cream
Toasted almonds

Heat the oven to 375°F, 190°C, Gas 5. Grease and flour an 8-inch (20-cm) diameter, 1½-inch (4-cm) deep cake tin (one with a removable base is a help).

Beat the margarine and sugar together until light, then add one egg at a time, together with a sprinkle of the flour, beating each egg in hard. Add the coffee and beat again. Finally fold in the rest of the flour and salt, quickly and lightly. Turn into the cake tin, make a slight hollow in the centre, and put the cake in the oven to bake for about 35 minutes or until the mixture has shrunk away from the sides of the tin, and does not dent when pressed with a finger.

Cool the cake in the tin, loosening it but not removing it until cold. Prick the cake thoroughly all over with a fork.

Meanwhile make the syrup by dissolving the brown sugar in the coffee over a low heat, then raising the heat and boiling for 5 minutes. Stir in the marsala and leave to get cold. Pour this syrup over the cake and leave for 24 hours (you can freeze it at this stage).

Cover the cake with the whipped cream and decorate with the almonds.

Chocolate and Chestnut Meringues

Any meringue recipe is useful for entertaining, as meringues will keep indefinitely in a plastic box with a well-fitting lid, and can be made when you have used the egg yolks for mayonnaise. This recipe is very useful if you want a dessert for a formal occasion.

Preparation time: 10 minutes

Cooking time: 4 hours

8 oz (225 g) caster sugar
1½ oz (35 g) cocoa
4 egg whites, at room temperature
1 × 14-oz (400-g) can chestnut purée, unsweetened
½ pint (300 ml) double cream
4 tablespoons caster sugar

Line a baking sheet with non-stick Bakewell paper and heat the oven to 300°F, 150°C, Gas 2.

Sift the sugar and cocoa together, making sure they are well mixed. Beat the egg whites until foamy, add a spoonful of the sugar mixture and continue to beat until the whites are stiff and stand in peaks. Fold in the rest of the sugar and cocoa quickly and lightly with a metal spoon.

Put tablespoons of the meringue mixture on the baking sheet. Bake low down in the oven until firm, turn them over carefully and replace them in the switched-off oven. They should be slightly chewy in the middle, not chalky like commercial meringues. They will probably take about 4 hours to cook, but much depends on the freshness of the eggs.

Turn the chestnut purée into a bowl, add the cream and about 4 tablespoons caster sugar (check that the purée is unsweetened). Beat well with electric beaters to break down the canned purée into a smooth, light cream.

Sandwich the meringues together with this mixture only 30 minutes before serving, and serve with extra single cream for pouring if you feel it necessary.

Makes 16 large meringues.

Frankie's Sugared Avocados

Make this in double quantities as it always proves popular.

Preparation time: 10 minutes

Cooking time: 15 minutes

2 avocados
Juice of 1 lemon
2 oz (50 g) soft brown sugar
3 tablespoons sweet sherry
Soured cream, chilled
Sponge fingers

Heat the oven to 375°F, 190°C, Gas 5, and butter a shallow ovenproof dish.

Halve the avocados, remove the stones and peel the fruit carefully. Cut into slices lengthwise, and sprinkle generously with lemon juice to stop them browning. Arrange the avocado slices in the buttered dish, sprinkle with the sugar and sherry and bake for 15 minutes.

Serve warm with chilled soured cream and sponge fingers.

Basic Pancakes

Pancakes are a useful stand-by; make them when you have time, layer them with Bakewell paper, wrap well and freeze them. They can be used with any number of fillings.

Preparation time: 5 minutes (1 hour in advance)

Cooking time: 10 minutes

½ pint (300 ml) milk
4 oz (100 g) flour
2 eggs
1 tablespoon caster sugar
1 oz (25 g) melted butter
Lard

Put all the ingredients except the butter in the blender. Blend for 1 minute and leave to stand for 1 hour.

Heat a small heavy frying pan and, as it heats, add the ounce of melted butter to the batter and blend again.

Melt a scrap of lard in the frying pan, and when it smokes pour in a small ladle of the batter, tilting the pan so that it covers the base. When the batter has set, turn the pancake carefully and cook the other side.

Continue until the batter is used up, layering each pancake as it comes from the pan with a piece of Bakewell paper. Freeze or store in the fridge until needed.

Makes 12 small pancakes

Pancakes with Brandy Butter

Fill the pancakes in advance and heat through when required.

Preparation time: 10 minutes

Heating time: 20 minutes

12 pancakes, made as in preceding recipe
Mincemeat, blackcurrant jam or apple purée
Brandy butter (page 111)

Put a spoonful of your chosen filling in the middle of each pancake, roll them up carefully and arrange, join down, in a buttered gratin dish. Dot with brandy butter (liberally) and heat in the oven for 20 minutes at 375°F, 190°C, Gas 5.

Pancakes with Raspberry Butter

A good dessert for a chilly summer evening, or a winter menu.

Preparation time: 10 minutes

Heating time: 20 minutes

12 pancakes, as before
Raspberry butter (page 111)
Caster sugar
Chilled whipped cream

Layer the pancakes and raspberry butter in a shallow gratin dish, sprinkling the top pancake with caster sugar. Heat for 20 minutes at 375°F, 190°C, Gas 5 and serve with the whipped cream.

Autumn Pudding

Make well in advance. The elderberries give a particularly subtle smoky flavour to the apple, so try to find some if you can. Even city dwellers are likely to find them – growing wild on building sites.

Preparation time: 10 minutes (24 hours ahead)

Cooking time: 15 minutes

6 oz (175 g) elderberries or blackberries
1¼ lbs (about 600 g) cooking apples, peeled and sliced
3–4 oz (75–100 g) sugar
½ pint (300 ml) water
Slices from a stale white loaf
Whipped cream

Stew the fruit with the sugar and water until soft, but don't overcook.

Line a 2-pint (1-litre) pudding basin with the slices of bread, first having removed the crusts. Pour in the fruit and cover the top with another slice or two of bread. Fit a wet saucer on top, with a weight on top of that, and leave in a cool place for 24 hours.

Turn out carefully and serve with plenty of whipped cream.

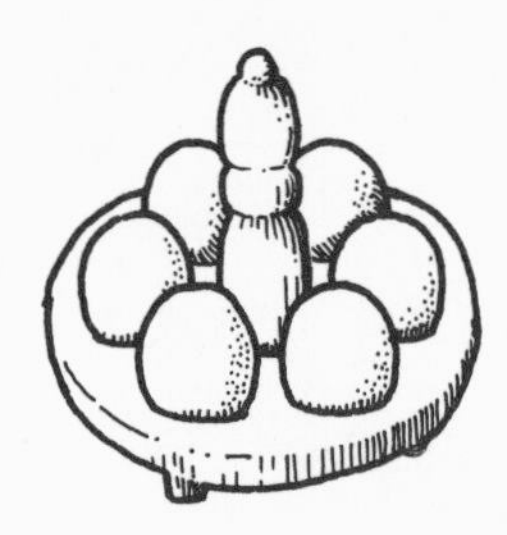

Angel Cake with Blackcurrant Purée

This is another useful cake to have in the freezer. It's very easy to make and goes well with any soft fruit.

Preparation time: 15 minutes + 5 minutes

Cooking time: 35 minutes + 10 minutes

2 oz (50 g) plain flour
3½ oz (90 g) caster sugar
6 egg whites, at room temperature
Pinch salt
¾ teaspoon cream of tartar
2¾ oz (60 g) caster sugar
½ teaspoon vanilla essence

Purée

1 lb (500 g) blackcurrants (frozen ones are fine)
6 oz (175 g) caster sugar
1 rose-scented geranium leaf or 1 tablespoon rose water
½ pint (300 ml) whipped cream, to garnish

To make the cake, heat the oven to 375°F, 190°C, Gas 5. Sift together the flour and the first lot of sugar, twice.

In a large bowl beat the egg whites, salt and cream of tartar with an electric beater until frothy. Add the second lot of sugar and continue to beat until you have a stiff meringue mixture. Fold in the sifted flour and sugar mixture and the vanilla essence quickly and lightly and pour into a hinged cake tin (a ring mould is best). Bake for 35 minutes, or until firm.

Cool the cake in its tin upside down on a cake rack – it will practically fall out when cold. Use at once or freeze until wanted.

To make the purée, cook the blackcurrants very gently with the caster sugar and the geranium leaf or rose water for about 10 minutes or until soft – don't add any water.

To assemble, split the angel cake in two horizontally and spread with the blackcurrant mixture (if you have used a ring mould, pour the purée into the centre of the cake). Reassemble and cover the entire cake with whipped cream.

Cherryfield Tartlets

I find this recipe invaluable. It was given to me by a friend whose life is so busy it makes mine seem like a perpetual holiday. These tartlets are perfect weekend food, can be served as a dessert (drink a chilled sweet white wine with them) or for tea, or taken on picnics. Double quantities are perfect for large buffets as they can be eaten easily with the fingers. I don't bother to freeze them, as they will keep well in an airtight box.

Preparation time: 30 minutes

Cooking time: 30 minutes

Pastry

12 oz (375 g) flour
4 oz (100 g) hard margarine
2 oz (50 g) pastry lard
1 dessertspoon vanilla sugar
Cold milk to mix

Filling

2 eggs
Pinch salt
6 oz (175 g) caster sugar
3 oz (75 g) currants
1 oz (25 g) melted butter
2 oz (50 g) chopped walnuts
1 oz (25 g) chopped dates
1 teaspoon vanilla essence

Make up the pastry in the usual way and chill in the fridge until needed. Heat the oven to 350°F, 180°C, Gas 4.

To make up the tartlets, roll out the pastry thinly and use to line greased bun tins, cutting the pastry with a large biscuit cutter. Put the tins in the fridge to chill the pastry while you make the filling.

Beat the eggs with the salt until pale and frothy, then add the sugar by degrees, still beating. When the mixture is thick, fold in the other ingredients. Put a generous teaspoon of this mixture into each pastry case – it will rise, so don't overfill – and bake for about 30 minutes, or until the filling is set and a biscuity brown.

Serve cold or warm. Makes about 24.

Dried Apricot Fool

Dried fruit is useful for winter puddings, but go out of your way to find fruit dried by natural processes as the flavour is incomparably better. Health-food shops are the best sources of supply. This apricot fool can be made in advance and kept in the refrigerator.

Preparation time: overnight + 10 minutes

Cooking time: 20 minutes

1 lb (500 g) natural dried apricots
½ pint (300 ml) water
4 oz (100 g) pale brown sugar
2 tablespoons marsala or apricot brandy
½ pint (300 ml) whipping cream
¼ pint (150 ml) soured cream

Soak the apricots in the water overnight.

Next day, cook the soaked apricots in their liquid for 20 minutes or until they are soft. Drain the fruit and purée in a blender or food-mill with the sugar and alcohol. Whip the creams together and fold into the purée.

Serve the fool in tall glasses with ratafias or macaroons.

Dried Fruit Salad

Preparation time: overnight + 5 minutes

Cooking time: 45 minutes

8 oz (225 g) hunza apricots (whole with stones)
4 oz (100 g) dried chestnuts
4 oz (100 g) dried apple rings
4 oz (100 g) dried peaches
2 oz (50 g) raisins
1 pint (600 ml) cold strained china tea
3 oz (75 g) brown sugar
Grated rind and juice of 2 oranges

Soak the dried fruit in the cold tea overnight.

Next day, strain the fruit, reserving the cold tea. Pick out the chestnuts and simmer them for 15 minutes in the tea (the fruit will have absorbed a good deal, so add some water). Then add the rest of the fruit and the sugar and simmer for about 30 minutes until soft.

Leave to cool, adding the grated rind and juice of the oranges about 30 minutes before serving.

Serve chilled, with whipped cream.

Rhubarb Glory

Preparation time: 10 minutes

Cooking time: 15 minutes

1 lb (500 g) young rhubarb
Grated rind and juice of 2 oranges
3 oz (75 g) demerara sugar
½ pint (300 ml) whipping cream
1 × 5-fl oz (150-ml) carton plain yoghurt

Trim the rhubarb and cut it into 1-inch (3-cm) lengths. Poach these very gently in the orange juice and sugar until tender (if you cook it too fast it will disintegrate and lose its lovely colour).

Cool, then spoon into tall glasses. Whip the cream with the orange rind and fold in the yoghurt, pile on top of the rhubarb in each glass and top with a sprinkling of demerara.

Serve with the Dessert Biscuits (page 112), flavoured with ginger.

Orange Trifle

Preparation time: 20 minutes

Cooking time: 5–7 minutes

1 packet sponge cakes (or 1 home-made sponge cake)
½ pint (300 ml) frozen orange juice
1 tablespoon Cointreau (optional)
4 large oranges
4 tablespoons caster sugar
½ pint (300 ml) whipping cream

Arrange the sponge cakes in a bowl and pour the orange juice, mixed with the Cointreau (optional), over them. Leave to soak while you prepare the oranges.

Peel the oranges carefully, removing all the pith with a sharp knife, then slice thinly, removing any pips as you go. Arrange on top of the sponge cakes.

Put the sugar in a heavy saucepan over a low heat until the sugar melts. Raise the heat and cook until a rich brown caramel. Take it off at once and pour over the orange slices. Whip the cream and pile some in the centre of the trifle, serving the rest separately.

Strawberries and Chambéry

Preparation time: 5 minutes (1 hour ahead)

1 lb (500 g) fresh strawberries
Vanilla sugar
Large glass Chambéry (best of all, use Sainsbury's strawberry Chambéry)

Hull and halve the strawberries, sprinkle with vanilla sugar to taste and pour the Chambéry over the top.

Serve chilled.

Cream Cheese and Fresh Pineapple

Quick to assemble – and delicious.

Preparation time: 15 minutes

8 oz (225 g) cream cheese
3–4 tablespoons thick cream
1 tablespoon Kirsch
Caster sugar
1 small fresh pineapple

Beat the cream cheese and the cream together, with the Kirsch and sugar to taste, until smooth. Cut the pineapple into neat pieces, removing all bits of core and skin, and sprinkle with more caster sugar.

To assemble, pile the cream mixture into glasses or dishes and top with the pineapple.

Lemon Creams

Make Lemon Creams 24 hours in advance to give them time to set. This is an ideal dessert to serve after a heavy main course.

Preparation time: 5–10 minutes

Cooking time: 15 minutes

3 lemons
6 oz (175 g) vanilla sugar (see page 112)
½ pint (300 ml) water
6 egg yolks
Whipped cream
Mint leaves

Grate the rind and extract the juice from the lemons. Put the grated rind and the juice into a bowl with the sugar and water. Whip the egg yolks until frothy, then fold them into the lemon mixture. Stand the bowl over a pan of hot water on a low heat and beat with electric beaters until thick. (You can do this in a heavy pan if you are brave – it is quicker, but you do run the risk of curdling the mixture). Cool, then pour the lemon cream into small bowls or glasses.

Before serving decorate with whipped cream and mint leaves.

Raspberry Sorbet

The rose water in this recipe enhances the summer aroma of this popular dessert. It makes a refreshing end to a winter meal, too, using frozen raspberries; they can be liquidised while still frozen.

Preparation time: 10 minutes + 5 minutes

Cooking time: 5 minutes

Freezing time: 12 hours minimum

2 lbs (1 kg) raspberries
Juice of 1 lemon
1 tablespoon triple-strength rose water
8 oz (225 g) vanilla sugar
½ pint (300 ml) water
3 egg whites, at room temperature

Liquidise the raspberries with the lemon juice and rose water.

Dissolve the sugar in the water over a low heat, then boil for 5 minutes and leave to cool. Add this syrup to the raspberry purée and pour into a plastic box. Freeze, uncovered, until the mixture is mushy.

Whip the egg whites until stiff. Pour the half-frozen raspberry mixture into a chilled basin and whip until fluffy, then combine with the whites. Return to the freezer, covered this time, and freeze until firm.

Eton Mess Ice-cream

Ice-cream recipes can be made when you have time and used when needed. Take the ice-cream out of the freezer and put it in the fridge for an hour before serving to let the flavours 'warm' a little.

Preparation time: 10 minutes

Freezing time: 12 hours minimum

1 lb (500 g) strawberries
1 tablespoon lemon juice
2 oz (50 g) caster sugar
½ pint (300 ml) double cream
½ pint (300 ml) whipping cream
6 meringues, roughly crushed

Hull the strawberries and mash them with a fork, mixing in the lemon juice and sugar. Whip the creams together until thick and fold in the strawberry mixture, adding the roughly crushed meringues. Mix well and freeze for at least 12 hours, stirring once or twice.

Orange and Lemon Ice-cream

Very good – and more economical than the Eton Mess Ice-cream.

Preparation time: 10 minutes

Freezing time: 12 hours minimum

4 large eggs, at room temperature
4 oz (100 g) vanilla sugar (see page 112)
½ pint (300 ml) double cream
Grated rind and juice of 1 lemon
Grated rind and juice of 1 orange
1 tablespoon triple-strength orange flower water

Separate the eggs, putting the whites in a large bowl and the yolks in a smaller one. Whip the whites until foamy, fold in a tablespoon of the sugar and continue to whip until the whites are stiff. Fold in the rest of the sugar to make a meringue mixture.

Beat the yolks until frothy. Beat the cream with the grated rinds and juices (it won't curdle, the acid helps thicken the cream). Then mix all the ingredients lightly together. Pour into lidded containers and freeze for at least 12 hours, but without stirring.

Fresh Peach Melba

This should be put together at the last minute. A good dessert for formal dinner parties. Serve in pretty shallow bowls which will show off the beautiful colours of the fruit.

Preparation time: 10 minutes

1 lb (500 g) raspberries
2 oz (50 g) caster sugar
4 fresh peaches
8 oz (225 g) vanilla ice-cream, home-made if possible.

Put the raspberries and sugar in the blender and blend to a purée. Peel the peaches by first dipping them briefly into boiling water, halve them, remove the stone, place in serving glasses and fill the cavities with ice-cream – and spoon a little more around. Mask with the raspberry purée and serve with wafers or boudoir biscuits.

Yoghurt Syllabub

Excellent for an informal buffet party.

Preparation time: 10 minutes + overnight

¼ pint (150 ml) double cream
¼ pint (150 ml) whipping cream
3 tablespoons sweet sherry
½ pint (300 ml) plain yoghurt
Caster sugar to taste

First chill all the ingredients in the fridge, then whip the creams into the sherry. Fold the yoghurt in last and add sugar to taste. Pour into glasses and leave overnight, or for 24 hours.

Yoghurt Fruit Salad

Make in advance and keep in the refrigerator until required. There are many variations on this theme, using fruit in season. Honeydew melon does very well, so do kiwi fruit, fresh pineapples, peaches and strawberries. But keep to the orange and lemon flavoured yoghurt as a base, and don't be tempted to use commercially flavoured yoghurt instead as it makes a mockery of the other fresh fruit flavours.

Preparation time: 15 minutes

2 oranges
2 oz (50 g) caster sugar
Juice of 1 lemon
1 × 1-pint (600-ml) carton natural yoghurt
4 oz (100 g) white grapes
1 Ogen melon

Peel and chop the oranges and stir the pieces with the sugar and lemon juice into the yogurt. Halve and de-seed the grapes (peel them, too, if you have time). Halve the melon, scoop out the seeds and chop the melon flesh roughly. Fold the grapes and melon into the yoghurt and serve chilled in small glass bowls.

Iced Cheese

Delicious as a formal summer dinner party savoury.

Preparation time: 10 minutes (24 hours ahead)

8 oz (225 g) any blue cheese, at room temperature
¼ pint (150 ml) double cream
Sunflower oil
About 1 oz (25 g) medium oatmeal

In a food processor, or in a bowl using electric beaters, blend the cheese with the cream – it shouldn't need any extra seasoning.

Oil a large margarine tub and sprinkle thickly with the oatmeal, shaking out any surplus. Press the cheese mixture into this and freeze for 24 hours.

An hour before serving, press the cheese out on to a plate and leave in the fridge.

Serve with warmed oatmeal or Bath Oliver biscuits.

STORE CUPBOARD

One or two useful things to make when you have time, which can be brought out of the larder to add interest to a meal.

RECIPES

Quick Spiced Cherries
Plum Sauce
Damson Chutney
Nerine's Pickled Beetroot
Salad Cream
French Dressing or Vinaigrette
Chopped Parsley
Forcemeat Balls
Garlic Bread

Pastes
Smoked Fish Paste
Turkey and Ham Paste
Pinwheels or Party Sandwiches
Brandy Butter
Raspberry Butter
Vanilla Sugar
Praline
Dessert Biscuits

Quick Spiced Cherries

Half a cinnamon stick
Scrap of whole nutmeg
6 black peppercorns
Piece dried ginger
¼ pint (150 ml) red wine vinegar
3 oz (75 g) raisins
1 × 15-oz (425-g) can stoned black cherries

Tie the spices in a clean handkerchief and put in a pan with the vinegar, raisins and drained syrup from the cherries. Bring to the boil and simmer for 10 minutes. Add the cherries and simmer for a further 5 minutes. Take off the heat and cool.

Remove the bag of spices and store the cherries and their syrup in screw-top jars (make sure the lids are plastic, not metal, as vinegar corrodes metal lids).

Keep at least a week before eating and serve cold with gammon or cold game, or hot as a sauce for roast game.

Makes 1 large Kilner jar.

Plum Sauce

2 lbs (1 kg) plums
2 large onions
½ pint (300 ml) cider vinegar
½ oz (12 g) salt
1 oz (25 g) pickling spice, tied in a clean handkerchief
4 oz (100 g) brown sugar

Halve and stone the plums, then put all the ingredients except the sugar into a pan and simmer until the plums and onions are soft – about 30 minutes. Purée in a liquidiser, return to the pan and stir in the sugar. Return to the stove and simmer for another 45 minutes, stirring every so often, until the sauce is thick.

Pot in warm dry jars. Useful for barbecue sauces, devils and curries.

Makes 2 × 8-oz (225-g) jars.

Damson Chutney

3 large onions
4 lbs (2 kg) damsons
2 lbs (1 kg) cooking apples
1½ pints (900 ml) cider vinegar
12 oz (375 g) brown sugar
1 dessertspoon salt
1 oz (25 g) pickling spice

Peel and slice the onions and put them in a large pan with the damsons. Roughly chop the apples (don't bother to peel and core them) and add them to the pan with the vinegar. Cook until soft and mushy, then push through a coarse sieve or through the coarsest screen of the food-mill. Return to the pan with the sugar, salt and spices (tied in a clean cloth) and simmer fast for 20 minutes or until thick.

Put in warm dry jars. Keep at least a month before eating.

Makes about 6–7 lbs (2.75–3 kg).

Nerine's Pickled Beetroot

Good enough to eat with bread and butter and wonderful in ham or cheese sandwiches.

1½ lbs (750 g) cooking apples, peeled and cored
2 enormous onions, peeled and sliced
1 level teaspoon ginger
1 level teaspoon salt
1 lb (500 g) sugar (use brown if preferred)
1 pint (600 ml) vinegar
3 lbs (1.5 kg) cooked beetroot, diced

Put all the ingredients except the beetroot into a large pan and simmer until the onion and apple are soft. Stir in the diced beetroot and cook until thick – about 20 minutes. Eat within 6 months.

Makes about 6 lbs (2.75 kg).

Salad Cream

Good for sharpening up cream dressings, and mayonnaises.

1 oz (25 g) flour
2 tablespoons sugar
2 teaspoons salt
1 tablespoon Dijon mustard
¼ pint (150 ml) water
¼ pint (150 ml) wine vinegar
1 oz (25 g) butter
1 large egg, beaten

Put the flour, sugar and salt in a pan and stir in the mustard, water and vinegar. Bring to the boil, stirring well, and simmer for 10–15 minutes. Add the butter and beat until it has melted. Put the egg into the blender and pour on the hot mixture, beating as you do so.

When cold, store in a jar in the fridge, where it will keep indefinitely.

French Dressing or Vinaigrette

Use only the best ingredients for this. If you prefer a mildly flavoured olive oil, buy it from Boots. I don't use sea-salt except at table, finding ordinary kitchen salt quite adequate for cooking – as long as it has none of the additives you find in 'table' salt.

6 tablespoons olive oil
1 tablespoon wine or cider vinegar, or lemon juice in certain cases
Salt and freshly ground black pepper

Put all the ingredients together in a screw-top jar and shake thoroughly before adding to the salad ingredients.

You can add any flavouring you like: a crushed clove of garlic, a teaspoon of mustard, a *pinch* of sugar, chopped fresh herbs (not dried, which just taste dusty). Try to make fresh dressing every time. It doesn't take a minute and the flavour is much better.

Chopped Parsley

Chopped Parsley makes a delicious extra seasoning to serve with most things – try having a bowl of it on the table, along with the salt and pepper mills, to sprinkle over your food. Parsley freezes well: simply pull the leaves from the stalks, put them in a plastic bag and freeze. The parsley can be crumbled in your fingers while it is still frozen.

Forcemeat Balls

Forcemeat Balls help stretch stews in a more original way than dumplings or potatoes. Mix the dry ingredients in double or triple quantities and store in the freezer – simply binding with an egg when you want to make the balls.

6 oz (175 g) fresh white breadcrumbs
4 rashers streaky bacon, chopped
3 oz (75 g) suet
Grated rind of 1 lemon
2 tablespoons chopped parsley
Pinch dried thyme
Salt and pepper
1 large or 2 small eggs, to bind
Dripping

Combine the dry ingredients and bind with the beaten egg. Form into balls. Fry in plenty of hot dripping until golden on all sides, drain on kitchen paper and serve separately on a warmed plate (not in the casserole) so that they keep their crispness.

Garlic Bread

Garlic Bread is always popular and it is worth making up two or three loaves at a time, wrapping them in foil and storing them in the freezer. Put them straight into the oven to warm up, ready to serve with a casserole or pâté (give the average French loaf about 40 minutes in a moderate oven). Make Curry Bread to serve with spicy dishes by adding curry paste or powder to the butter.

Pastes

Pastes made from cooked fish and meat are often glorified with the name of 'pâtés', which they are not. They are very good in their own right, and good to serve as first courses, as sandwich fillings, and as breakfast dishes instead of the more usual bacon and eggs. A food processor makes very short work of preparing them. Here are two basic recipes which can be varied as much as you like.

Smoked Fish Paste

8 oz (225 g) cooked flaked smoked fish: haddock, kippers, trout, mackerel, herring
2 oz (50 g) butter, at room temperature
Pinch mixed spice
Pinch cayenne
Pepper, salt if necessary
Clarified butter, to seal (see page 43)

Remove any bones from the fish, then beat all the ingredients together until smooth and pot as for Turkey and Ham Paste (next page).

Serve with hot toast and lemon wedges, or in sandwiches.

Turkey and Ham Paste

1 lb (500 g) cold roast turkey
4 oz (100 g) cooked ham
4 oz (100 g) butter, at room temperature
Nutmeg, salt and pepper
Clarified butter, to seal (see page 43)

Mince the meats together (or process for about 30 seconds) and beat in the butter and seasonings (season well, as the paste can be too bland). Pot in a china jar, and seal with a thick layer of clarified butter.

This paste will keep for about a week in the fridge, but once the seal is broken, eat within 24 hours.

Pinwheels or Party Sandwiches

Roll out crustless slices of very fresh brown bread with a rolling pin and spread them generously with one or other of the above pastes (extra butter is not needed). Roll up as tightly as possible, wrap in foil and chill in the fridge for 2–3 hours. Cut in slices about ½ inch (1 cm) thick, using a very sharp bread knife.

Bring to room temperature before serving, as cocktail or pre-prandial snacks. They freeze well, of course.

Brandy Butter

Brandy Butter will keep for months in the fridge and makes a delicious sauce for many hot puddings – not just Christmas pudding.

8 oz (225 g) brown sugar
1 lb (500 g) unsalted butter
2 sherry glasses brandy
Grated rind of 1 orange
Grated nutmeg

Put all the ingredients in a heavy pan over a low heat and stir frequently as the butter melts. As soon as it has, beat hard until the mixture is smooth. Put the pan in a cool place and stir the butter every so often as it cools. When cold, beat again and store in margarine tubs in the fridge.

Raspberry Butter

Raspberry Butter makes a good filling for pancakes (see page 99) and cakes.

4 oz (100 g) unsalted butter, at room temperature
10 oz (300 g) vanilla sugar
12 oz (375 g) fresh or frozen raspberries
2 oz (50 g) ground almonds

Beat the butter and sugar together, then add the raspberries and finally the almonds. Beat to a cream and store in the fridge. Use within 2–3 weeks, as the oil in the almonds, and the butter, will go rancid if kept for too long.

Vanilla Sugar

Vanilla Sugar is so easy to make that you need never be without it. Bury vanilla pods, cut into 2-inch (5-cm) lengths, in a jar of caster sugar, topping up with more sugar as you use it and giving the jar an occasional shake. Be generous with the vanilla pods – I use 3 whole ones to a jar which holds 1 lb (500 g) sugar. The pods can be bought from good grocers, and they last for months.

Praline

Praline is another invaluable storecupboard standby, which will enhance ice-creams, syllabubs, trifles and cakes.

4 oz (100 g) hazelnuts or unblanched almonds
4 oz (100 g) vanilla sugar

Put both ingredients in a heavy pan over a low heat and cook gently until the sugar melts. Raise the heat and cook until the sugar caramelises, tipping the pan every so often so that the nuts are well coated. As soon as the mixture is a rich brown, pour it on to a lightly oiled baking sheet and leave until quite cold. Break into pieces and drop these one at a time on to the whirling blades of the blender through the hole in the lid. You can do it all in one go in a food processor. Store the praline powder in a screw-top jar.

Dessert Biscuits

This biscuit dough can be flavoured to suit whatever you want to serve the biscuits with – ginger to go with dried fruit salads and rhubarb dishes; nuts to go with soft fruits; almond or vanilla essence to accompany syllabubs.

4 oz (100 g) soft margarine
7 oz (200 g) caster sugar
Pinch salt
8 oz (225 g) plain flour
2 teaspoons baking powder
1 egg

Cream together the margarine, sugar and whatever flavouring you choose. Mix the salt, flour and baking powder together. Beat the egg into the creamed sugar and margarine, with a spoonful of the flour, then work in the rest of the flour.

Form into a roll about 2½ inches (5 cm) in diameter, wrap in foil and chill in the fridge until you are ready to use the dough (you can freeze it at this point, if you wish).

Shave off thin slices with a sharp knife and arrange them on a greased baking sheet. Cook for 10 minutes at 350°F, 180°C, Gas 4, until crisp and pale brown. Lift off with a palette knife while still warm and cool on a rack.

PARTY DRINKS

You can simply serve red or white wine at a buffet or wine and cheese party, the choice depending on your pocket and palate. As an alternative, try these party drinks.

RECIPES

White Wine Cup
Kirs and Cardinals
Mulled Wine

White Wine Cup

An excellent summer drink.

2 bottles dry white wine
1 glass brandy
Peel of half a cucumber
1 bottle soda water, chilled
Sprigs of mint

Mix the wine, brandy and cucumber peel and leave to stand for 30 minutes. Add the chilled soda water and garnish with mint.

Makes about 10 glasses.

Kirs and Cardinals

Lovely cheap party drinks.

A Kir, *or* vin blanc cassis, *is simply a tablespoon of* crème de cassis *in a large wine glass, topped up with a chilled dry white wine.*

A Cardinal *is the (naturally) red version – again, the same amount of* crème de cassis *topped up with a light red wine. Beaujolais is ideal.*

Mulled Wine

My recipe uses no brandy, which minimises the risk of a hangover. Do use whole spices if you can; ground ones make a very dusty drink.

For a mulled wine and mince-pie party after carol singing or a Christmas pantomime, prepare the mulled wine and mince-pies before you go out, leave the wine in the slow-cooker on low, and put the pies in the oven, setting the oven-timer to come on 30 minutes before your return, at about 300°F, 150°C, Gas 2.

½ pint (300 ml) water
1 cinnamon stick
Half a nutmeg
1 whole orange stuck with 6 cloves
2 tablespoons brown sugar
2 bottles full-bodied red wine (a Rhône, Spanish Rioja, or Sainsbury's red Bergerac)

Bring the water, spices and orange to the boil, then stir in the sugar until dissolved. Add the wine and heat until *about* to boil (don't let it), then strain it into a jug for serving, leaving the spices behind to re-use for the next helping (you will have to add more sugar, of course).

A slow-cooker is ideal for mulled wine as it will keep the wine at the right temperature until you are ready to serve it. Bring the water and spices to the boil as before, then add the sugar and wine and pour it all into the crock-pot; have it on high if you are in a hurry, or leave it on low for a longer period.

Makes about 10 glasses.

COOKED-AHEAD MENUS

These consist of dishes prepared (although not necessarily cooked) in advance, needing only the finishing touches. They need forethought, but will enable you to spend more time with your guests.

SPRING

Raj Creams (*page 32*)
Lamb Cutlets Portmanteau'd (*page 57*)
Spring Cabbage with Tarragon (*page 84*)
Frankie's Sugared Avocados (*page 98*)

SUMMER

Lettuce soup (*page 22*)
Seviche (*page 46*)
Brown Rice, Red Pepper and Onion Salad (*page 92*)
Cucumber and Yoghurt Salad
Raspberry Sorbet (*page 104*), and Almond Dessert Biscuits (*page 112*)

AUTUMN

Pâté Maison (*page 28*)
Fish Lasagne(*page 45*)
Chicory and Egg Salad (*page 85*)
Orange and Lemon Ice-cream (*page 105*)

WINTER

Rillettes (*page 28*)
Goulash and Dumplings (*page 60*)
Brown Rice
Buttered Carrots
Pancakes with Brandy Butter (*page 99*)

QUICK-ASSEMBLY MENUS

I suggest these menus for informal entertaining as they leave you with little organising to do ahead of time, but quite a lot to do at the last minute. Useful for spur-of-the-moment invitations, if you can shop on the day.

SPRING

Stir-fried Spiced Liver (*page 62*)
Pitta Bread
Mixed Salad

Cheese

Rhubarb Glory (*page 102*)
Boudoir Biscuits

SUMMER

Chilled Avocado Soup (*page 24*)

Grilled Mackerel on Fennel (*page 47*)
New Potatoes
Broad Bean Salad (*page 80*)

Fresh Strawberries

AUTUMN

Quick Mushroom Soup (*page 22*)
Fillet of Pork with Mustard and Cream (*page 55*)
Buttered Rice
Runner Beans

Yoghurt Fruit Salad (*page 106*)

WINTER

Oeufs en Cocotte with Garlic Butter (*page 34*)
Fiery Duck (*page 69*)
Sweet and Sour Beetroot (*page 81*)
Cream Cheese and Fresh Pineapple (*page 103*)

TROUBLE-FREE MENUS

Here is a combination of cooked-ahead dishes, quick-assembly dishes, and dishes which can be left to cook largely on their own.

SPRING

Mushroom Paste (*page 36*)
Rabbit and Pork Casserole (*page 72*)
Baked Potatoes
Broccoli
Cherryfield Tartlets (*page 100*)

SUMMER

Raw Smoked Haddock (*page 31*)
Shoulder of Spring Lamb with Lemon and Herbs (*page 53*)
Gratin Dauphinois
Green Salad
Angel Cake and Strawberries (*see page 100*)

AUTUMN

Lebanese Aubergine Salad (*page 35*)
Chinese Roast Duck (*page 69*)
Brown Rice
Chrysanthemum Salad (*page 86*)
Pancakes and Raspberry Butter (*page 99*)

WINTER

Celery Soup with Stilton (*page 24*)
Braised Venison (*page 71*)
Boxty (*page 91*)
Buttered Carrots
Coffee and Marsala Cake (*page 96*)

INFORMAL MENUS

Ideas for after-cinema or theatre suppers, Saturday lunches, high teas.

SPRING

Cold Herb Omelettes (*page 33*)
Risi e Bisi (*page 77*)
Cheese

SUMMER

Bagna Cauda with Raw Vegetables (*page 37*)
Spaghetti di Rinforza (*page 74*)
Raspberries

AUTUMN

Potatoes à la Ritz (*page 90*)
Cold Ham
Celeriac Salad with Tomato Mayonnaise (*page 85*)
Fruit

WINTER

Potato Soup (*page 23*)
French Bread Pizzas (*page 76*)
Yoghurt Syllabub (*page 105*)

FORMAL MENUS

These are menus for when you want to impress, or celebrate. You will need to allow extra time, but the menus I have suggested here are not too demanding.

SPRING

Creamy Ham Rolls (*page 30*)
Crisped Turkey (*page 68*)
Braised Fennel with Parmesan (*page 86*)
Potato Purée with Carrots (*page 90*)
Lemon Creams (*page 103*)

SUMMER

Sweetcorn, Mushroom and Crab Soup (*page 23*)
Stroganoff Salad (*page 59*)
Brown Rice, Red Pepper and Onion Salad (*page 92*)
Fresh Peach Melba (*page 105*)

AUTUMN

Prosciutto and Pears (*page 30*)
Gougère of Shellfish (*see page 40*)
Green Salad
Iced Cheese (*page 106*) with celery
Dried Fruit Salad (*page 102*)

WINTER

Consommé and Caviare (*page 33*)
Irish Fillet of Beef (*page 52*)
Jerusalem Artichoke and Potato Ragoût (*page 80*)
Chicory and Egg Salad (*page 85*)
Chocolate and Chestnut Meringues (*page 97*)

BUFFET MENUS

When organising a buffet, remember that whether people sit down to eat or not depends entirely on what you give them. No one can manage a knife and fork, glass and plate, standing up. Even if you can provide some tables (see page 19), make the food simple enough to be eaten with a fork alone, or with fingers (this will save washing-up, at least).

SPRING

Eggs with Tuna Stuffing (*page 30*)
Pork and Spinach Moussaka (*page 61*)
Yoghurt Syllabub (*page 105*)
Dessert Biscuits (*page 112*)

SUMMER

George Hardie's Omelette Cake (*page 74*)
Various salads
Angel Cake (*page 100*)
Strawberries or Raspberries
Cheeses

AUTUMN

Creamy Ham Rolls (*page 30*)
Chicken Saunders (*page 65*)
Cherryfield Tartlets (*page 100*)

WINTER

Beef and Kidney Stew (*page 58*)
Curry Bread (*page 110*)
Orange Trifle (*page 102*)
Cheeses and Celery

WEEKEND MENUS

These menus are devised to combine keep-warm dishes for late arrivals, cooked-ahead recipes, and food for children, over a weekend.

WINTER

Friday Supper: Goulash and Dumplings (*page 60*)
Dried Fruit Salad (*page 102*)

Saturday Lunch: Fish-in-the-Hole with Tomato Sauce (*page 42*)
Fresh Fruit

Saturday Dinner: Oeufs en Cocotte with Garlic Butter (*page 34*)
Leg of Lamb with Green Peppercorns (*page 52*)
Gratin Dauphinois
Watercress Salad
Coffee and Marsala Cake (*page 96*)

Sunday Lunch: Cold Lamb
Baked Potatoes
Alfalfa and Carrot Salad (*page 94*)
Damson Chutney (*page 108*)

Sunday Supper: Risi e Bisi (*page 77*)
Cheese and Fruit

WEEKEND MENUS

When planning menus for summer weekend guests, include dishes which can easily become picnic food.

SUMMER

Friday Supper: Portuguese Fish (*page 44*)
Rice
Salad
Strawberries and Chambéry (*page 103*)

Saturday Lunch: Salad Niçoise (*page 77*)
Cheese

Saturday Dinner: Green Peppers Stuffed with Tomatoes and Anchovies (*page 92*)
Shoulder of Pork with Fennel Seeds (*page 54*)
Golden Potatoes (*page 89*)
French Beans
Eton Mess Ice-cream (*page 104*)

Sunday Lunch: Cold Pork
New Potato Salad
Cheese

Sunday Supper: Pasta with Fresh Herbs and Parmesan

EMERGENCY MENUS

From the list of items for the larder on pages 11–13, I have created some sample menus to cover the occasions when you haven't even time to defrost anything from the freezer.

Fresh fruit and cheese are the obvious endings to this sort of meal, but you can draw on your stocks of canned black cherries, pineapple, or bottled fruit. Good quality ice-cream kept in the freezer will stand you in good stead. Try a combination of chocolate ice-cream with hot black cherries: strain the syrup from the cherries into a pan, add a teaspoon of cornflour mixed with a little cold water, a tablespoon of brandy (or, better still, Kirsch), a pinch of cinnamon and a couple of cloves; simmer all together until thick, then add the cherries and let them heat through before serving with the ice-cream. Canned chestnut purée, whizzed in the blender with a little milk or thin cream to give it a thinner, smoother consistency, and sweetened to taste if using the unsweetened variety, goes deliciously with coffee ice-cream.

SPRING

Eggs with Tuna Stuffing (*page 30*)
Tagliatelli and Ham (*page 75*, using canned ham)

SUMMER

Canned consommé, either hot (with a little sherry) or cold (garnished with any fresh herbs)
Spaghetti di Rinforza (*page 74*)

AUTUMN

Sweetcorn, Mushroom and Crab Soup (*page 23*)
Risi e Bisi (*page 77*)

WINTER

Oeufs en Cocotte with Garlic Butter (*page 34*)
Frankfurters and Sauerkraut

WINE & CHEESE PARTY MENUS

Keep the food as simple as possible, and serve it on large plates on a central table.

SUMMER

Rillettes (*page 28*) or Simple Pâté Maison (*page 28*)
on rounds of French bread

Anchoïade (*page 36*) or Bagna Cauda (*page 37*) or Mushroom Paste (*page 36*)
as dips with bread sticks, Ritz crackers or Sainsbury's sesame crackers

French Bread Pizza (*page 76*)
cut into bite-size pieces

Raw Smoked Haddock (*page 31*)
on squares of brown bread and butter

WINTER
(in addition)

Chilled Avocado Soup (*page 24*, but without the milk and using Tabasco instead of chilli peppers) as a dip for hot sausages on sticks

Cumberland Sausage, cut into mouthfuls
served hot on sticks,
or cold with Nerine's Pickled Beetroot (*page 109*) as a dip

STOCKISTS

I would like to pay tribute to the role played (unwittingly) by both Marks and Spencer and Sainsbury's in the compiling of this book. As a working housewife and living as I do in the north of England, I would not have been able to find all the ingredients so easily and so quickly had I not been lucky enough to have branches of both shops within reasonable reach. Marks and Spencer are particularly good at supplying well-trimmed meat for instant cooking – expensive, but totally without waste (much regretted by the dog); Sainsbury's have a larger range, and best of all, fresh herbs and interesting vegetables. Both shops yield good wines too, as I mentioned at the beginning of the book.

For strange spices like green peppercorns (although Sainsbury's now stock these) and star-anise, I went to Culpeper Ltd. They have several branches and a good mail order service (Hadstock Road, Linton, Cambridge). Luckily dried spices and herbs weigh light, so the cost of postage is not a problem.

For kitchen equipment, David Mellor Ltd was an obvious choice as they now have a branch in Manchester as well as their main shop in Sloane Square. Their stock of basic equipment is large and comprehensive, and I don't think you need look anywhere else for good saucepans, knives, and oddities like timers on a string to hang round your neck, ceramic pastry beans, and wooden forks for stirring cooking rice, and hooking pasta out of boiling water – a notoriously difficult culinary task.

For electrical equipment such as slow-cookers and whisks, your local discount warehouse is as good a place as anywhere.

INDEX

Numbers in bold type denote a main recipe

alfalfa and carrot salad **94,** 121
anchovies 12, **35**
  anchoïade **36**
  bagna cauda **37**
  green peppers stuffed with **92,** 122
apple
  autumn pudding **99**
  purée **70,** 99
apricots, dried 12, 102, 119
  fool **101**
artichokes, jerusalem **80,** 119
aubergines **35,** 117
avocado
  dip **124**
  salad **94,** 115
  soup **24,** 116, 124
  sugared **98**

bagna cauda **37,** 118, 124
barbecues 20, 108
bean shoots **94**
beans
  broad **80,** 116
  flageolet **67,** 68, **87**
  french **34**
  haricot **56**
beef 11
  and kidney stew **58,** 120
  gamed steak **56**
  goulash **60,** 115
  Irish fillet **52,** 119
  roast wing rib **51**
  stroganoff salad **59**
beetroot **81,** 116
  pickled **109,** 124
  salads **82**
  soup **24**

biscuits, dessert 102, **112,** 115, 119, 120
blackberries **99**
blackcurrant purée **100**
brandy butter 99, **111,** 115
bread
  curry **110,** 120
  French, pizza **76,** 118, 124
  garlic **110**
  pitta 24, 62, 116
  sauce **66**
broccoli **83**
Brussels sprouts 71, **83**
buffets 19, 30, 61, 65, 85, 87, 92, 100, 105
  menus for 120
butter
  brandy 99, **111,** 115
  to clarify **43**
  garlic **34,** 116
  raspberry 99, **111,** 117
  savoury 50

cabbage
  red **70**
  spring **83, 84,** 115
cakes
  angel **100,** 117, 120
  coffee and marsala **96,** 117
  omelette **74,** 120
capon, braised **68**
carrots 51, **84,** 90, 94, 119, 121
cauliflower 83, **84**
caviare 20, **33, 90,** 117, 119
celeriac **85,** 117
celery **68, 87**
  soup **24,** 117

cheese
  boursin 33
  cream 37, 76, 103, 116
  iced **106,** 119
  Parmesan 68, 76, 86, 119
  Stilton **24,** 117
cherries 13, **108,** 123
Cherryfield tartlets **100–1,** 117, 120
chestnut purée 12, 20, **97,** 119, 123
chicken 40, 42, **56,** 61
  braised **64**
  cold 87
  joints **64**
  livers **29**
  pollo tonnato **67**
  roast **66**
  Saunders **65,** 120
chicory and egg salad **85,** 115, 119
chocolate
  ice-creams 123
  meringues 20, **97,** 119
chutney, damson **108,** 121
cod **41, 46,** 47
coffee
  ice-cream 123
  and marsala cake **96,** 117, 121
coley **44, 45, 46**
cooked-ahead menus 115
consommé 12, **32,** 123
  and caviare 20, **33,** 119
crab 12
  mushroom and sweetcorn soup **23,** 119, 123

dabs 40
damson chutney **108,** 121
desserts 95–106
  biscuits 102, **112,** 119, 120

duck **69,** 116, 117
dumplings **60,** 121

eggs 11
  in chicory salad **85,** 115, 120
  oeufs en cocotte **34,** 116, 121
  omelettes **33, 34, 74,** 118, 120
  pipérade **35**
  stuffed **30,** 119, 123
elderberries 99
emergency menus 123

fennel
  braised **86,** 119
  raw **37,** 87
  seeds **54,** 122
  stalks **47,** 116
fenugreek **94**
fish 11, 39–47
  casserole **46**
  fishes and cream **40**
  fish-in-the-hole **42,** 121
  foil-baked **41**
  lasagne **45,** 115
  Portuguese **44,** 122
  seviche **46,** 115
  smoked **110**
  see also individual entries
flageolets **68, 87**
flan, pipérade 35
forcemeat balls 56, **110**
formal entertaining 20, 86, 97, 105
  menus for 119
frankfurters 12, 123
French
  bread 110, 124
  pizza **76,** 118, 124
  dressing **109**
fruit salad
  dried **102,** 119
  yoghurt **106**

game 11, 63–72
  see also individual entries
garlic 12, **71**
  bread **110**
  butter **34,** 116
  and onion purée **64**
  tomato sauce **44**
gougère **40**
  of smoked haddock **40–1,** 119
goulash **60,** 115, 121

grapefruit **38**
grapes, in yoghurt fruit salad **106**
grouse, devilled 20

haddock 33, **40, 42, 45,** 46
  gougère of smoked **40–1**
  raw smoked **31,** 117, 124
  scalloped, with watercress **31**
ham **75, 80, 87,** 109, 123
  creamy ham rolls **30,** 119, 120
  and turkey paste **111**
  proscuitto 13, 33, **38,** 119
hare, Corsican **71**

ice-cream **105,** 112, 123
  Eton mess **104,** 122
  orange and lemon **105,** 115
iced cheese **106,** 119
informal menus 118

kidneys, beef **58,** 120
  lambs' **58**
kiss-me-quick pudding **96**
kiwi fruit 106

lamb 11, 61
  cutlets portmanteau'd **57,** 115
  with green peppercorns **52–3,** 121
  with lemon and herbs **53,** 117
  ragoût **59**
leeks **84, 88**
lemon **53,** 71, 117
  creams **103,** 119
  and orange ice-cream **105,** 115
lettuce soup **22**
liver, chicken **29, 64**
  lambs' **62,** 116

mackerel **47,** 116
melon **38, 106**
menus
  buffet 120
  cooked-ahead 115
  emergency 123
  formal 119
  informal 118
  quick assembly 116
  trouble-free 117
  weekend 121–2
  wine and cheese party 124
meringues 20, 97, **104,** 119
mincemeat 99

moussaka **61,** 120
mushrooms 7, **64, 76, 83,** 116, 117,
    119, 123, 124
  croûtes **32**
  paste **36**
  salad **82**
  soup **22, 23**
  stir-fried **94**

oeufs en cocotte **34**, 116, 121, 123
olives 12, 35
omelettes **33, 34,** 118, 120
  cake **74,** 120
onions 12, **88, 92,** 119
  purée **64**
orange-flower water 36, 96, 105
oranges **55, 106**
  ice-cream **105,** 115
  pork chops with **55**
  trifle **102,** 120

parsley, chopped as a condiment
    110
pancakes **98, 99,** 115, 117
pasta 12, 42, **45, 74, 75, 76,** 115,
    117, 123
pastes **110–11**
  choux **40**
  mushroom **36,** 117
  smoked fish **110**
  turkey and ham **111**
pâté 20, **28,** 115, 124
peaches **105,** 106, 119
pears **37, 38,** 119
peas 77, **88**
peppers **91, 92,** 119, 122
pheasant **70**
pickled beetroot **109,** 124
  cucumber **26**
picnics 19–20, 100
pigeons **70**
pineapple, canned 13, 123
  fresh **103,** 106, 116
pinwheels **111**
pipérade **35**
pitta bread 24, 62, 116
pizza 20, **76,** 118, 124
plaice **43**
plum sauce **108**
pollo tonnato 19, **67**
poppadoms 32

pork 11, **28, 29, 56**
  chops with oranges **55**
  with fennel **54,** 122
  fillet **55,** 116
  moussaka **61,** 120
  and rabbit casserole **72,** 91, 117
  rillettes **28,** 115, 124
potatoes 52, 53, 55, 66, 71, **80,** 85, **89, 90, 91,** 117, 119, 122
  baked, à la Ritz **90,** 118
  devilled **90**
  and pepper galette **91**
  soup **23,** 117
praline **112**
puddings 95–106
pulses 12

rabbit and pork casserole **72,** 117
raj creams **32,** 115
raspberries **105,**
  butter 99, **111,** 117
  sorbet **106,** 115
ratatouille, canned 13, **35**
rhubarb **102,** 116
rice 12
  brown **92,** 115, 119
  risi e bisi **77,** 118, 121
rillettes **28,** 115, 124

salad cream **109**
salads 33
  avocado and fenugreek **94**
  aubergine **35,** 117
  beetroot **82**
  broad bean **80,** 116
  brown rice and red pepper **92**
  cauliflower **84**
  celeriac **85,** 117
  chicory **85,** 115, 119
  chrysanthemum 68, **86,** 117
  cold pasta **74–5**
  dried fruit **102,** 119
  fennel **87**
  flageolets **87**
  Niçoise **77,** 122
  omelette **34**
  stuffed peppers as a **92**
  stroganoff **59,** 119
  yoghurt fruit **106**
salmon 41
sauerkraut 13, 124
sausages **56,** 87, 124
seviche **46,** 115
shellfish
  chowder **25**
  prawns 7, **30, 32,** 33, 40, **80,** 119
  shrimps **43, 45**
smoked fish paste **110**
sole **40**
sorbet, raspberry **106,** 115
sorrel 33
soups
  avocado, chilled **24,** 116, 124
  beetroot, cold **24**
  celery **24,** 117
  leek and pea **88**
  lettuce **22,** 115
  mushroom **22,** 116
  potato **23,** 118
  shellfish chowder **25**
  sweetcorn, mushroom and crab **23,** 119, 123
  watercress, and tomato **25**
spaghetti di rinforza **74,** 117
spinach 29, 33, **61, 74, 93,** 120
sprouting seeds for salads **94**
Stilton and celery soup **24,** 117
stir-fried spiced liver **62,** 116
  mushrooms and bean shoots **94**
strawberries **103, 104,** 106, 122
sweetcorn 13, **23,** 119, 123
syllabub **105,** 118, 120

tagliatelli **76**
terrine, pork and spinach **29**
tomatoes **25, 34, 74, 92,** 121
  mayonnaise **85**
  sauce **42, 44**
trifle, orange **102,** 120
trouble-free menus 117
trout 41, **43**
tuna 12, **30, 67, 75,** 87, 120, 123
turkey, crisped **68,** 119
  and ham paste **111**
turnips, in lamb ragoût **59**

vanilla sugar 105, 106, **112**
venison **71,** 117
vermicelli, with cream cheese and mushrooms **75**
vinaigrette **109**
  leeks, **88**
vin blanc cassis **114**

watercress
  and tomato soup **25**
  and scalloped haddock **31**
weekend entertaining 19–20
  menus 121–2
white wine cup **114**
whiting 46
wine and cheese party menus 124

yoghurt fruit salad **106,** 116
  syllabub **105,** 118, 119, 120
Yorkshire pudding **51**